The Costa Rica Escape Manual

Nadine Hays Pisani

www.happierthanabillionaire.com

The Costa Rica Escape Manual 2019 / Nadine Hays Pisani -- 1st ed.
ISBN: 9781790341368

Dedication

To that beautiful person dreaming of a different life.

Books

- *Happier Than A Billionaire: Quitting My Job, Moving to Costa Rica, & Living the Zero Hour Work Week*
- *Happier Than A Billionaire: The Sequel*
- *Happier Than A Billionaire: An Acre in Paradise*
- *The Costa Rica Escape Manual* Editions

Connect with Me

- www.facebook.com/happierthanabillionaire
- www.happierthanabillionaire.com
- www.instagram.com/happierthanabillionaire
- www.youtube.com/happierthanabillionaire
- www.twitter.com/happierwithless

email: puravida@happierthanabillionaire.com

Contents

Spreading Roots

Working in Costa Rica

Buying Property

Blathering

Road Trips

Acknowledgments

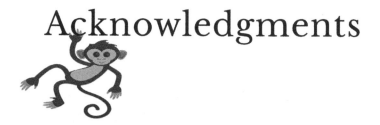

I could not have completed this book without the interviews from these exceptional people: Marcia, Gilfred, Barry, Daniel, Dervin, Alex, José, Ale, Aaron, Alejandro, Tim and Kim, Cathy, Kimberly, and Stephanie and Ben. Thank you for contributing your time to this edition. Your guidance is invaluable to all those preparing for their own move to Costa Rica.

To my parents, thank you for telling me that the world is too big to stay in one spot. I'm lucky to have you in my life, and I will continue to fix all your computer problems. And Mom, Facetime is definitely on your iPad. The Apple store did not sell you one without it.

To my sister Stacey, go to Mom's house and show her where the Facetime app is on her iPad.

And to Rob, who knew my prince would come in the form of a poor boy from Bensonhurst, Brooklyn?

There is no other kingdom I wish to live in.

"Reading gives us someplace to go when we have to stay where we are."

~Mason Cooley

Lake Nicaragua
NICARAGUA
San Juan del Sur
Penas Blancas
Los Chiles
Golfo de Papagayo
Liberia
Play Hermosa
Coco
Liberia International Airport
Arenal Lake
Sugar Beach
Playa Potrero
Flamingo
Arenal Volcano
Caribbean Sea
Playa Grande
Tamarindo
Tortuguero
Avellana
Playa Negra
Monteverde
Poas Volcano
Naranjo
Sarchi
La Paz Waterfall Gardens
San Ramon
Grecia
Ostional
Nosara
Alajuela
San Jose
Puerto Limon
Atenas
Samara
Juan Santamaría International Airport
Escazu
Cahuita
Santa Teresa
Mal Pais
Puerto Viejo
Punta Uva
Jaco
Playa Hermosa
Manzanillo
Playa Bejuco
Sixola
Manuel Antonio
San Isidro del General
Dominical
Uvita
PANAMA
Pacific Ocean
Rincon
Drake
Puerto Jiménez
Paso Canoas
Carate

Map

Paper Airplanes

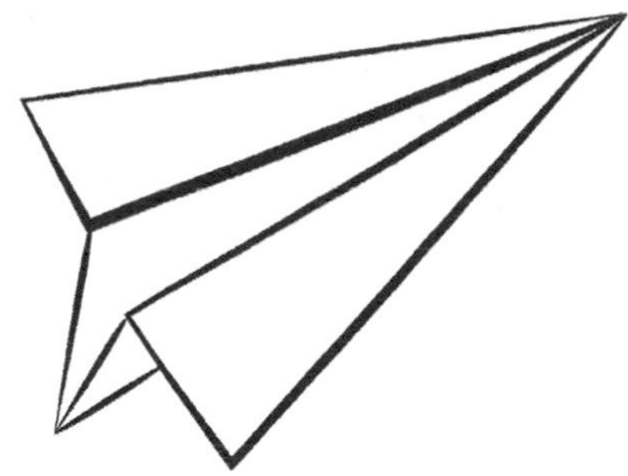

"Don't live the same year seventy-five times and call it a life."

~ Robin S. Sharma

This book is filled with information gathered by someone who has lived happily in Costa Rica for over ten years. Some of these topics may not pertain to you. That's okay. You don't have to move here forever. You can come for a sabbatical, stick your toes in the sand, and recall what it's like to live without acid reflux, ditching those tension headaches for the sound of the ocean lapping at your feet.

That's what this book is all about, helping others to love a place so much it changes who they are. It's what this country did for me, and for most of the expats I know. Some say it's the people, others say it's the beautiful surroundings. I say it's because I was ready. Ready for an adventure. Ready for a life outside the office that was all but suffocating me.

Expatriating to Costa Rica is much like flying a paper airplane. You follow the steps, fold all the seams perfectly, and wait for a strong gust of wind. But when you release it into the air, it veers sharply to the left. You return to the drawing board and tweak your plans, maybe even getting tips from one of NASA's leading wind engineers. Surely, nothing can go wrong now! But once tossed, your creation dramatically spins in a circle before landing at your feet.

Just then a surfer comes along and haphazardly folds the paper three times before giving it a try. Remarkably, it takes flight, catches a breeze and disappears into the distance. He smiles, grabs his board, and runs off toward the beach, never once thinking about what he did right or wrong.

That's why it's important to remember that results may vary. It's also a funny phrase my husband came up with while I was writing the first *Escape Manual*. It's a theme you'll start to understand well as you read through this book, one that my father never wanted me to write.

"They're heavy, boring, and awkward," he said. "The pages get dog-eared, and once you make the supreme effort to read it, there's nothing but a dull textbook quality. On and on they drone. In the end, all travel guides end up in the corner of one's garage." Believe it or not, he considered this a pep talk.

I want this book to be your most powerful tool for navigating a happy life in Costa Rica. So to make this version of the *Escape Manual* the best one ever, and ensure it's not relegated to a corner of your garage, I have taken all of your suggestions into consideration and included many of them in this edition.

New Additions to the Manual

Checklists!

Everyone loves a checklist, but not my husband. He constantly forgets them at home and ends up calling from the grocery store, asking, "Do we need tomatoes?" Yes, Rob, we need tomatoes, but *you'll* never wonder if you need tomatoes because now there's a checklist for everything built right into this book: getting residency, flying with pets, opening a bank account, and running to the border will now be as easy as "check one, check two, check three."

Rental Car Confusion

I receive many emails asking about rental cars. A number of third-party sites entice travelers with advertisements offering cars for as little as $7 per day. What a bargain! You get ready to pony up the cash, only to be charged ten times that amount once you arrive at their office. In order to clear this up, I reached out to a company that doesn't do this, Vamos Rent-A-Car. Their operations manager shares everything you need to know in the chapter, "Renting a Car."

And yes, there is a checklist for that too!

Residency

We'll talk with our residency specialist, attorney Marcia Solis from Send Me South. She understands the ups and downs of this process and shares with us new residency laws, the reasons to file, and when not to file; she even provides a checklist of everything you'll need to get started.

Dental Tourism

That's right, the exciting topic of affordable teeth cleaning, wisdom tooth extraction, and other oral procedures. We'll hear from Michelle and her spouse, Ben, who traveled to Costa Rica on a joint vacation and dental adventure. My husband calls this a two-for-one excursion. I call it a great way to save money while also enjoying a holiday abroad.

Building, Buying, or Developing Property

If you're considering purchasing land in Costa Rica, these chapters are a must-read. I can't stress enough how important it is to understand the complexities of the laws surrounding real estate in Costa Rica. For this edition, I dove in deep, like middle-earth deep. And then I took a shovel and dug a little more. Once there, I discovered information that many potential buyers need to know before building, buying, or even developing raw land from scratch.

Working in Costa Rica

Can you work legally? We'll go through the requirements needed to get that much-sought-after work permit and introduce you to a variety of people making a living in Costa Rica. They're a fun bunch, rich in enthusiasm and eager to share what they've learned.

Road Trip

Take a road trip with me! From the northwest beaches in Guanacaste all the way to the Osa Peninsula, we'll explore the sights together and you'll understand why I fell in love with Costa Rica. Although this chapter is not a substitute for a *Frommer's* travel guide, it's a wonderful introduction to the many places I've written about in my previous books and includes beautiful pictures.

Index

This is the first version of the *Escape Manual* with an index (print edition only). Now you can easily navigate throughout this book! If you're reading this on a phone or tablet, just use the search option for any inquiry. To test it out, search for "Kung Fu hamster," a nod to all those people who emailed me and told me they bought one too. They even sent pictures. It warms my heart to know that other adults have frivolously squandered their money on a nunchuck-swinging robotic rodent.

The only differences between the print and e-book versions are that the latter is in color and has clickable links while the paperback has an index and markable checklists. Both the print and digital version will be handy when visiting the country, for different reasons. I love when people show me their *Escape Manual* with dog-eared pages and notes written throughout! My dad would be proud.

Blathering

People familiar with my writing know I tend to go off on silly tangents. It's because I see all of you as my friends, sitting across from me, drinking a cup of coffee, and discussing my crappy car. And that's what my books are all about. Facts, anecdotes, and stories of my husband telling me it's perfectly reasonable to drive a vehicle while things are falling off the engine.

However, it's been made clear that my blathering irritates certain people. My sincere apologies. So I took those random rambling chapters and grouped them all into one Blathering section, making it easy for that certain someone to skip right past it. And for that adorable little curmudgeon who wrote a stinging review about my last edition, the chapter entitled, "Don't Share This Book" is dedicated to you. You're recorded in the index, under *My Dad Doesn't Like You*. There is no checklist.

Come along for the ride and see why my husband and I call this beautiful country our home. We've certainly run into our share of problems, some small, others big, and one that was colossal. But we're still here, still married, and still happier. Some may be secretly researching this move. And perhaps you've only recently mentioned it to your spouse, like Jim. He just turned to his wife, Hazel, and said, "Let's move to Costa Rica!"

"You're crazy," she replied. That's okay. Every relationship has the crazy one. In mine, that would be my husband, Rob. I'm the more pragmatic one, which means the non-fun one, which means the never-be-late one.

I'm early for everything while Rob is always forty-five minutes late. He's sloppy; I'm neat. He wanted to move to Costa Rica. I told him to drop it. That's until I realized I couldn't live the rat race anymore. Rob was right all along; there is so much more of this world to explore, and sometimes it takes a nudge to get you going on that grand adventure. We all have grand adventures waiting to unfold.

"See, Hazel? These two idiots moved to Costa Rica," Jim says. "Why can't we?"

It's true, Hazel, these two idiots did do it. We also built The Happier House, and you can read that story in my latest book,

Happier Than A Billionaire: An Acre in Paradise. It chronicles that funny year with stories about our daily challenges, Rob's ridiculous building ideas and a strict budget that left us struggling to come up with unique solutions. It was nuts, folks. But we did build a beautiful place where couples stay and ask us questions about how they can do it too.

I'm going to teach you how to make paper airplanes. It requires no special equipment, just patience, a good sense of humor, and the acknowledgment that most of them will land at your feet. It's based on the balance of four aerodynamic concepts: weight, drag, thrust, and lift. We'll go through each of these principles, and in no time you'll be launching your own airplane.

Let's take a journey toward bubble-gum-colored sunsets and deserted beaches, to a place where you can hear howler monkeys roaring across the rainforest canopy. And to Jim, tell Hazel you're going to take her on a vacation where you'll kiss her under a waterfall. And don't phone this one in, Jim. Kiss her the way you did when you first met.

You'd be surprised how persuasive a kiss from a good man can be.

Links:

Nunchuck-Swinging, Robotic Hamster:
https://youtu.be/-t49FkbZRUI
Coffee Video: https://youtu.be/aafFTs-1GIM
Monkey Alarm Clock Video: https://youtu.be/TSQQ6XMBjpc

The Starting Line

Paper Airplanes

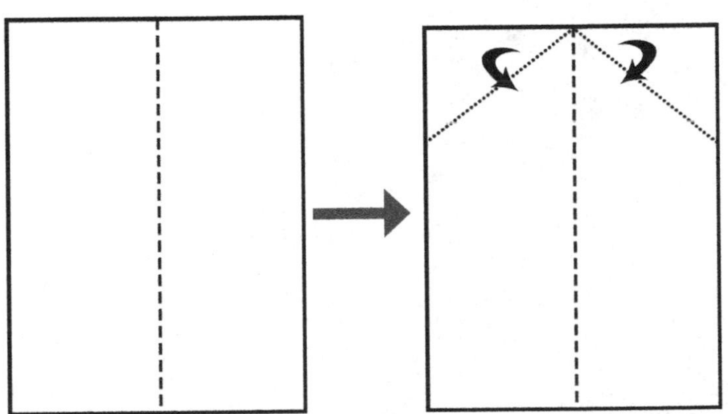

Crease middle of paper

Fold each of top corners to center line

Howler Monkey

How It All Begins

"If everyone waited to become an expert before starting, no one would become an expert."

~ Richie Norton

What is your immediate plan? Are you hiding this book from your spouse, not yet ready to tell him or her you want to move to Costa Rica? Or are you close to retirement and looking for a place to escape the cold winters? Having an idea of where your starting line is will help you make the best decisions regarding this dream.

If you know about my story, you know that we escaped from a stressful life. I'm not sure how I conjured up the courage to quit and sell everything at thirty-seven and move to a country where we didn't understand the language, knew no one, and had no idea on what to do for employment. It was reckless, ridiculous, and romantic. I wouldn't trade that decision for the world.

You may feel the same way but want to be a bit more prepared than that Happier couple who threw every safety net into the wind. So ask yourself, where are you in your life? Are you a happy person? Is your job so stressful you're holding on by a thread? If you can be honest and dig deep into your headspace, you'd be surprised the gems you'll uncover—ideas and solutions that will lay the groundwork for starting a new life in a new country.

Take a moment to develop a different plan for each of these scenarios:

1. A vacation.
2. Spending a month.
3. Spending three months (that way, you can leave before your visa runs out).
4. Spending half the year.
5. All In: the big move.
6. Or no move at all! Simply dreaming about it is good enough.

Go over each of these. Better yet, lie in bed with your spouse and dream about the possibilities for each. No stress. No demands. Just mind map a plan.

Vacation

Can you each get time off and take a vacation to Costa Rica? Can the kids get out of school for that length of time? Would it be an exploratory mission, or are you just so darn tired you want to sit in an infinity pool with a piña colada and stare at the sailboats? That's okay. We have plenty of people who stay at The Happier House that do just that. Sometimes the best vacation is doing nothing at all. Maybe you just want to see if this is a place that feels like home.

You can also decide if you want to stay at a resort or a private house. Many people choose resorts because that's the easiest, but why not step out of your comfort zone? Rent a house or condo for the week so you can see what it's like to actually live here.

Spend a Month

Is there is a possibility that you can extract yourself from work and spend a month in Costa Rica? Wow, that would be great. That gives you enough time to start living like a local (which is always cheaper than living like a tourist), soaking up the Pura Vida lifestyle, and taking more day trips than you would have if you were just here on vacation. But I warn you, the Costa Rica magic will begin to attach itself to your DNA, and you'll find it hard to leave.

Three Months

This is the best-case scenario if you would like to relocate. You can rent different places throughout the country and decide which location is right for you. There are many microclimates here, and you can test each one out and find the spots that make you the happiest. I would check out three places: the central valley, the Guanacaste coast, and the southern Pacific beaches. Each has its own vibe, climate, and different pros and cons.

Inevitably, you will land in a spot that feels great. Suddenly, you're not thinking about that neighbor back home who never rakes his leaves or that coworker who always dumps his work onto your desk. In fact, these things don't even get you angry anymore. Now that you have the Pura Vida chromosome, life is looking a heck of a lot brighter.

Half the Year

If you can do this, you are likely either retired or able to work remotely. I've met many people who only need a Wi-Fi signal to do their job. They can work at the top of a volcano or while swinging in a hammock. It may be possible to live a dual life, like an undercover agent. You're a beach bum half of the year but then get to go back home and continue your other life. But I can guarantee that half of the year will be dreaming about getting back to Costa Rica.

I'm All In!

Okay, you're the crazy bunch, and there are plenty of people like you living in Costa Rica. I should know because I'm one of them. The funny thing is that I shouldn't have been. I'm not a risk taker like my husband. I'm more pessimistic and cynical than he is. But there was a point in my life when I realized I was going to be stuck in that office until I was in my sixties if I didn't leave immediately. An epiphany occurred; a moment of clarity. Suddenly I was wide awake, and I wanted a change ... I needed a change.

If you go this route, you need to start thinking about how to unravel your complicated life. And I know it's complicated, because all of our lives are. You'll have friends and family telling you that you're crazy, you're having a midlife crisis, you're selfish, etc. All of it or none of it may be true. But if you want to do this, really want to give it a shot, you'll have to start making some big decisions. We'll get into that throughout the book.

The very first thing I want you to do is to look around and think about what you want to keep. If it's the person lying next to you and maybe a few pets, then you and I have everything in common. If you want to hold on to that crystal sugar bowl your sorority sister gave you for an engagement present, then you have a lot of decisions to make.

Rob and I sold everything because financially we had to, but also because I didn't want to straddle two different countries. If I had a foot left in the United States, it would have been easier for me to quit and go home whenever anything difficult came up. It's amazing how resourceful you are when your back is in a corner. Have you ever seen a cat fight its way out of a paper bag? Now imagine if the other end of the bag was open. There would be no reason to fight.

Or no move at all!

I like you already. You're someone who snuggles in bed with a book to enjoy a mental vacation. I do that every night. That's the joy of reading, and why we have books on our Kindle, crowding our nightstand, piled on bookshelves, and some boxed up but never given away. Bibliophiles get through life by funneling thousands of words into their brain every day. I hope this mental vacation leaves you with a smile on your face and a book that will not get relegated to the corner of your garage.

Crime: My Seven Lucky Rules

"Crime is common. Logic is rare. Therefore, it is upon the logic rather than upon the crime that you should dwell."

~ Sherlock Holmes

I place this information in front of the book so that it can be included in the free sample. If there is any chapter that I want you to remember from *The Costa Rica Escape Manual,* it's this one. I'm giving you my honest advice on how to avoid being a victim of crime.

I can think of a hundred factors other than crime that you should be considering before moving here. It shouldn't be the number one concern on your list, but it also shouldn't be the last.

I am a happy person living in a very happy country and have never been a victim of crime. But that may be because we take precautions. A lot of precautions. Some are reasonable, and some are nuts because I'm married to a guy from Brooklyn.

Vacationing Advice

Let's be honest: there is a lot of petty theft in Costa Rica. It stinks, but there are ways to mitigate your chances of getting robbed. Not surprisingly, if you leave your backpack lying on the beach unattended, chances are it will not be there when you get back. Recently, a woman I know left her wallet on the table at a restaurant. She walked away for ten seconds to take a picture, and it was gone when she returned. It happens that fast.

There are also skilled pickpockets in the touristy areas. They can easily unzip your purse while it's hanging on the back of a chair and snatch your wallet. They will reach into your pocket as well and steal your cell phone. This happens all the time, so you need to be very aware of your surroundings and what possessions you're carrying.

I know someone who decided to go skinny-dipping in the middle of the night and left her purse with her passport, rental car keys, cash, and credit cards on the beach. It wasn't there when she returned and neither was her clothing. Don't do that.

People say to always have your passport on you. Instead, I would recommend taking a picture with your phone of the front page with all your information and the page that was stamped at immigration. Police want to see that you haven't overstayed your 90-day visa. If you were to be pulled over by the police, I would show them those pictures. That way you can keep your passport back in the hotel room safe.

Everyone loves a beach day, but it's also an easy way to lose your stuff. For this reason, you should leave unnecessary things in the hotel room safe. The stickler is if you want to bring your cell phone to take pictures, but still want to go into the ocean.

Buy a waterproof bag and keep the phone with you. You'll see plenty of people using them at the beach. It's a perfect solution!

In my husband's attempt to thwart crime, he shoves our phone and keys into a waterproof Ziploc bag. He then buries them in the sand when no one's looking and places an unassuming coconut on top to mark the spot. Bravo, Robert! I applaud him for being so creative. Of course, when we return from our swim, every coconut looks the same. I like to call this "An Idiot's Scavenger Hunt." We end up spending the remainder of the day digging in the sand like two numnuts.

Even though the ocean breeze feels nice in the evening, do not sleep with your sliding doors open. Also, you'll be surprised how flimsy sliding door locks are, and how most are broken inside your room. My husband buys a bunch of broomsticks for a buck each in the grocery store and wedges them into the tracks. It's always fun walking into a hotel with them and being mistaken for the cleaning crew.

Car Advice

Breaking into cars is Costa Rica's number one recreational pastime, so take your bags into the restaurant with you. Don't be embarrassed by this; you'll see plenty of people doing the same thing. If you're not keen on taking all of your bags with you every time you stop, look for a place where you can watch your car the entire time you're eating.

I once locked my keys in my car, and two nice Ticos tried to help me get the car door open. After fifteen minutes, I noticed a teenager sitting twenty feet away laughing and shaking his head. I walked over and offered him five dollars if he could unlock my car. He grabbed a tool out of his bag and opened the door in under three seconds. I can't figure out any other comparable occupation that utilizes these skills except the precise one I hired the kid to do. He has quite the future.

⚠ Pay attention at gas stations. Another prevalent crime involves two or more people working together to distract you. Make sure you lock your car if you're going in for a snack. And never leave your purse unattended on the passenger seat, even if it's just to check your oil.

As for car theft, it does happen, but it's not as prevalent as your iPhone or computer getting stolen. Rob has installed three kill switches throughout our car, which basically makes it impossible for anyone to start it, including us. Do you remember the Club? We have two of them. On occasion, our car is more secure than the Pope-mobile. In fact, if the Pope-mobile ever did go on sale, Rob would be the first in line to buy it. Its bulletproof glass and climate-controlled interior would make for an excellent way to tour the country.

Stop Reading Here

If you read the *Happier Than A Billionaire* series, you know that my husband's hobby is crime prevention. He's not a professional crime fighter but a crime enthusiast. There was a big argument about including the following precautions that my husband submitted to the Happier writing department. The editor-in-chief carefully considered the list and decided that her husband was nuts. "No one wants to read this!"

But Rob insisted that these suggestions are a perfectly reasonable way to protect ones' property. So, to avoid any further arguments, I'm including them and calling the following the Macaulay Culkin, Costa Rican Home Alone Security System. Enjoy.

- Grow thick thorny bushes around your property.
- Run a line of clear fishing line with large, barbed fishing hooks throughout your bushes. Make sure to hang them above the height of any potential dogs or small animals.
- Connect solenoids to mouse traps. These are placed on your roof and trigger shotgun shell blanks when your alarm goes off. This all but confirms you'll never be invited to Taco Tuesday by your neighbor.
- Connect a smoke machine to your alarm and add cayenne pepper to the reservoir to unleash a fog that will mimic knockout gas on unsuspecting intruders.

- Use real and fake security cameras and motion sensors around the exterior of your home.
- Use battery-operated , wireless motion sensors or driveway alarms when staying at a temporary unsecured location.
- Post multiple laminated warning signs informing would-be intruders of the cameras, and include verbiage that lets them know that images are being uploaded and stored directly to the web. Video evidence is powerful in Costa Rica, and most criminals know this.
- Hide your belongings well when you're out of the home. Remove parts of furniture to place items in hidden recesses, or use large black kitchen bags to store items in the dirtiest, most inconvenient corner of your attic.
- Place items in a waterproof container dig a hole in the yard when no one is around, and bury valuables until you need them.
- Check window and door frames often. Crooks try to avoid breaking windows and will remove a few screws or rivets from an underused port of entry when you aren't at home.
- Finally, speak with a heavy Brooklyn accent when addressing suspicious characters. This might be the most powerful tool of all.

It's Safe to Start Reading Again

Wow, that was a mouthful. It's the reason I call our place the Thunderdome: two men enter, one man leaves. Please call before visiting.

After reading all that, you would think it's *The Walking Dead* around here. These ideas are crazy, but on the other hand, it could be the deadly fishhooks, exploding alarm sirens, disorienting knockout gas, bullet shells, and Brooklyn accent that has kept us safe for all these years. And in case you're wondering if my neighbors are doing the same thing, the answer to that is a resounding no. No, they are not. But if all this sounds good, Rob is available for any of your apocalyptic needs.

⚠ What's most important to take away from this chapter is that there is not a large police presence in Costa Rica, so personal responsibility is important. That's why you see fences around houses and bars on windows. It persuades crooks to consider another home, perhaps one without any security. Criminals are attracted to the path of least resistance. Either way, it's important to at least report any crime to the OIJ (Organismo de Investigación Judicial). Unfortunately, the closest police department may be an hour away.

In this country, alarms are never programmed to call the police since they may not show up, but you can easily have one programmed to call your cell phone. In the past, we hired a private security firm. But now, the development we live in has their own 24-hour security. This is a great way to feel safer in your home. It's nice to know that if anything happens, someone will show up.

Now that we've gone over my take on crime in Costa Rica, here's a recap of some rules Rob and I live by:

Seven Lucky Rules

1. Never leave any bags in the car.
2. Be mindful of the possessions you're carrying around with you. Don't leave purses hanging on the backs of chairs or cell phones hanging out of your pockets.
3. Always lock the doors to your house and car.
4. Do not sleep with windows or doors open on the first floor, or the second floor without reliable motion sensors to wake you up. I know that the ocean breeze feels nice, but too often it makes for an easy way for people to slip in and out without even waking you up. This is a common home invasion scenario. At first, it feels nice, like your spouse has cleaned up a bit. Until you realize it was burglars that were doing the cleaning.
5. Be careful at night, especially when leaving nightclubs.
6. If someone tells you a certain area is dangerous at night, believe them.
7. Most of all, always give the appearance that you're alert and aware of your surroundings, and if possible, turn on the Brooklyn accent.

These are my seven lucky rules, but I'd like to point out that for a place with such a small police presence—and no army—it is still known to be one of the happiest countries. I think that says a lot about the Costa Rican people.

Links:
OIJ agency for reporting crime: https://pj.poder-judicial.go.cr/
S.E.S Security Donald or Patricia | email: privatesecuity_ses1@hotmail.com

If you are in the Guanacaste area, Brian Howard is an excellent installer and supplier of alarms email: gtesecurity@gmail.com

Llanos de Cortés Waterfall

Vacation Packing CheckList

"A vacation is like love: anticipated with pleasure, experienced with discomfort, and remembered with nostalgia."

~ Evan Esar

- ☐ Passport.
- ☐ Sunscreen (very expensive here).
- ☐ Ibuprofen (very expensive here; Tylenol is much cheaper).
- ☐ Anti-itch medication (hydrocortisone, Benadryl, etc.).
- ☐ A pair of long pants that go down to your ankles. Shirt with long sleeves.
- ☐ Rain jacket and hat. A poncho is a cheaper approach, but I prefer a separate hat because a poncho hood always falls off my head when I look up.

- ☐ GPS: Pair your navigational tools (such as Waze) with a map.
- ☐ Water shoes.
- ☐ Mini flashlight.
- ☐ Batteries. I've bought some here that were dead on arrival.
- ☐ Sneakers for excursions that involve hiking, zip-lining, etc.
- ☐ Insect repellent. It's much more expensive here, especially in the tourist areas.
- ☐ Dry bag to put your cell phone in so you don't have to leave it on the beach when swimming.
- ☐ Phone (see phone chapter).

PacSafe Backpack. These bags have a cable running through them that you can secure around a tree, pole, or even sink plumbing in your hotel room.

At Llanos de Cortés waterfall, I saw a German tourist wrap a cable around a tree to secure his PacSafe backpack. He then went for a swim. Although I would never recommend leaving your items unattended, there will be moments when you'd love to take a dip in the ocean with your family or want to put your backpack in the overhead bin of a bus (thieves love this). When this cable is secured around a firm item, the person who is running at full speed to snatch the bag will get a nice and well-deserved whiplash injury.

Quick and Odd Tips

Tico Vernacular for a Costa Rican (male). Tica is the female equivalent.

Time Costa Rica is on Central Standard Time and does not use daylight savings time.

Tico Time A phrase used to describe the laid-back attitude here. No one arrives early, or on time, or even fifteen minutes late. We've waited entire days for repairmen. Also, getting the check in a restaurant is remarkably slow. If I had to choose, I would always pick Tico Time over the rat race I was accustomed to back in the United States. Tico Time may make you impatient, but it never gives you an ulcer.

Gringo A descriptive term for foreigners and rarely meant to be derogatory.

Green / Rainy Season The period from May through the second week in November.

Septic Systems It is frowned upon in some establishments to flush your toilet paper. Unfortunately, their septic systems are not suitable for it. If you see a wastebasket next to the toilet filled with paper, you can assume that's where the paper goes. Be nice, don't flush.

Suicide Shower Many economy rentals aren't plumbed for hot water, and you may rent a place that has a nifty donut-shaped piece of plastic covering the shower head with exposed wires jutting out. This is affectionately referred to as a suicide shower. It's used to heat water and can give you an unexpected jolt of electricity if you reach up to adjust it while in use. It's unnerving, but I've asked many Ticos if anyone has ever been fried by one and they just shrug their shoulders.

"To awaken quite alone in a strange town is one of the pleasantest sensations in the world." ~ Freya Stark

Restaurants Bills already include a 10% tip, but tip more if you think the service warrants it. People don't make a lot here, so a little extra goes a long way for these folks.

Water Generally, the water is safe to drink in Costa Rica. But be mindful and take precautions when necessary, especially near beaches and in very remote areas.

Parking Attendants Those guys you see wearing reflector vests and instructing you where to park are usually not legit. But they do provide a service, and I make it a habit to tip them. You may find that some want 500 colones or more. I will usually pay what they ask because they also watch your car. We didn't pay once, and we found our antennae yanked off when we returned. Some may call that extortion. I call it a gentle reminder that people are trying to make a living here.

Road Signs While driving, you will see signs with the town's name and the distance to your destination. Then, fifteen minutes past that sign, there will be another one stating the distance again, and it's even further! You have now officially entered the Tico Kilometer matrix.

Sodas are small Tico restaurants that sell comida típica (traditional Costa Rican food). If you drive past one that looks busy, don't hesitate to stop (but bring your bags inside or park where you can watch your car). They will surely have casados on the menu, a dish comprised of rice and beans, salad, plantains, and chicken or beef. It can cost as little as five dollars a plate!

Electricity Outlets are standard 110 volts. Although three-pronged outlets are available, older establishments may not have them. Bring an adapter if necessary.

Senior Citizens go to the front of the line in Costa Rica. So if you are one, Mick Jagger your way past everyone.

Credit Cards Although most credit cards are accepted in Costa Rica, some businesses can't swipe ones without raised digits. This can happen at your rental car agency. Call first and ask.

Money Don't bring ripped or raggedy money. It's tough to spend it here. Fifty- and hundred-dollar bills may also be harder to break, but you can certainly go inside a bank and do it there.

Rash Guards The perfect attire for snorkeling and spending time in the water. The sun is powerful here, and most people get burned (especially their feet). It's important to note that sunscreen kills the coral reefs.

Dates Written numbers and months are reversed. June 2, 2018 is written: 02/06/2018.

Blinking Headlights This may signify a road stop ahead, an accident, or any other reason you may want to slow down.

Left Turn Signal Signifies that the person in front of you is either turning left or wants to you to go around him. Think about the absurdity of that for a second. Choose wisely.

What About My Stuff?

"The ability to simplify means to eliminate the unnecessary so that the necessary may speak."

~ Hans Hoffman

We go through life collecting so many things, only to have them crowd our closets, cabinets, and shelves. Eventually, our stuff begins to weigh us down: first metaphorically, then physically when we decide to move. And weight is the earth's gravitational pull on a paper airplane. **If your paper is too heavy, it will never get off the ground.**

Relocating abroad puts everything you own under a microscope. What is it you truly need to be happy? You'd be surprised how little it is.

In my first book, I wrote about my robotic martial arts hamster. When you turned it on, it played "Kung Fu Fighting" while flamboyantly twirling nunchucks. I can't remember why I bought it; perhaps it was a gift for my husband. All I know is that it made me laugh. (I'm happy to say many readers have emailed me stating they too bought the Kung Fu robotic hamster. And they can't remember why they purchased it either.)

When contemplating our move, I stared at this hamster and realized I needed to untangle a very complicated life. I had to Kung Fu–chop items from my past to give me the freedom to move forward. My existential crisis didn't include a robotic hamster, so it was then that I decided everything had to go.

Rentals are usually furnished in Costa Rica, so there may not be any room for your furniture. And you need to consider if your furniture is appropriate for the climate. It's surprising how living in a rainy area can grow copious amounts of mold. I've owned leather belts that looked like Chia Pets after a month. Sometimes that perfect rental seems perfect until it isn't.

When we lived in Grecia, a cloud came through the house every afternoon. It was heavenly, and it subsequently left a heavenly layer of mold behind our cabinets, in our closets, and on my leather purses.

Now I live in Guanacaste, the driest area of the country, and don't have a mold problem. But I do have problems with the sun damaging furniture. These are things you can only learn once you live here, and it may persuade you to limit the items you are considering shipping.

This was also such a big move in my life, I needed to travel light. I just couldn't imagine renting a shipping container, arranging for its delivery, paying taxes on everything, and not being sure where we would land. It was overwhelming enough quitting my job and tossing my future into the unknown, I'm not sure if I could have added anything else to my plate.

And let's all be honest with ourselves: some of the happiest times in our lives were when we owned less. Remember the freedom of moving with one car load full of stuff? When was the last time you did that? There were no clipboards, itemized lists, packing tape, or eighteen-wheeler trucks. All you did was stuff your crap into garbage bags and shove it into the backseat and trunk of your vehicle. There is a lot to be said for being that mobile.

That's the strange thing about possessions. They feel good the moment you purchase them, but then that feeling quickly goes away. It's the desire of them that's the high, not the actual ownership. So once I figured that out, it was easier to start over.

Now that we built The Happier House, I still don't regret our choice of selling everything. What I owned in the United States would not have matched the new house, and the furniture would not have fit the scale of the rooms. But my neighbor shipped everything and is very happy. And I was happy too since she had so many appliances they gave me one of her many toasters.

Ask yourself these questions:

- Am I okay with living with less stuff?
- What are the things I can't live without
- Do I want to recreate my life in Costa Rica, or start a brand new one?

The last question is the most important. The people I see leave Costa Rica and move back home are usually people who wanted to recreate their life. They harped on the fact that they couldn't find the latest iPhone, or their favorite cheese, and nothing was as easy for them as it was at home.

All of that may be true. Things will be different here and some days will be incredibly challenging, but that was exactly what I was looking forward to. A different way of living.

The orange glow of adventure does not promise you a paved highway. It's filled with dirt roads riddled with potholes. But it's also here that once you let go of all your trappings you'll laugh the hardest, feel the best, and breathe the easiest.

For me, it all started with that Kung Fu hamster, but your situation may not be the same as mine. You may be building a house and want to ship everything. Congratulations! There is nothing wrong with having some of the comforts of home.

The next chapter will be all about the big move. Let's see if we can make it a smooth one.

I'm Keeping My Stuff

"That rug really tied the room together."
–The Dude, *The Big Lebowski*

If selling everything isn't the right choice for you, there's another option: the exciting world of international shipping! It's going to take some planning and work, but let's try to get your stuff down here successfully. Before we go into the long-winded explanation of the process of shipping your items, let's first discuss how people get their things to Costa Rica.

Expats love it when friends come to visit, but the reason is only half because they miss you. The other fifty percent is your suitcase real estate. It's as coveted as a Manhattan penthouse overlooking Central Park. I'm a normal person, so I'll ask my friends for easy-to-pack items like printer ink or index cards. My husband, on the other hand, will ask for a Weedwacker, and two SUV wheel hub assemblies, and four sets of brake pads, and ...

Flying: When flying, there is a tax exemption of $500 per person every six months on personal items. If you fill your suitcase with one hundred Yankees baseball caps, they may suspect you're hauling merchandise and planning on selling it. Be prepared to pay commercial tax on the hats. But normal, everyday things you can easily get through without any fees.

Online Shopping: It's important to note that this tax-exempt status also applies to products you order online and have shipped to Costa Rica. You just need to have someone file exoneration paperwork. This can cost upwards of $35, so it is best to reserve it for a big-ticket item. Results will vary with this, and sometimes it's just easier to pay the tax.

Amazon ships to Costa Rica and automatically includes import tax. Read the chapter, "Amazon.com: Are We Breaking Up?" for more delightful information regarding this topic.

Shipping Containers: Surprisingly, shipping containers are reasonably priced if you're looking to move a large number of possessions to Costa Rica. As a rule, plan to pay $1,500 for a twenty-foot shipping container, while a forty-foot container will cost closer to $2,000. But that's just for the container; there are plenty of other fees involved. Also, take into account that there will be charges to move your things to the nearest seaport, so all of this adds up quickly.

You can expect to pay approximately $6000 to $15,000 for a container measuring twenty to forty feet. That includes transportation costs and import tax.

If you want to ship a smaller amount, you can hire a freight consolidator. They'll lump several shipments together in their containers. This is more affordable. In both cases, you'll need to retrieve your items within 90 days of their arrival.

Let's assume that you've already moved to Costa Rica and are waiting for a shipment. At some point, you will need to get to customs to retrieve the items your wife packed into the shipping container. How did I know your wife was in charge of the packing? Because that's what we do unless we want the wedding china shoved under the Rubbermaid container full of automotive tools. Once at customs, things really get interesting. You might have to make a few trips to the customs office in San José, so make sure you have all your paperwork ready. You will need:

- A copy of the main page of your passport, as well as the page with the entry stamp from when you last entered Costa Rica.
- A detailed list of the contents of the container and their declared value.
- All the paperwork from the shipping company.

How do they determine the fair tax for each item? Well, look no further than the fascinating periodical called *The Interna-*

tional Convention on the Harmonized Commodity Description and Coding System (otherwise known as the HS Book).

The HS Book: The HS—as the cool kids like to call it—is the classification system that establishes the tariffs owed on each item. Although there are a few exceptions, everything gets taxed. Even your old Van Halen T-shirts.

I urge you to hire a customs broker to do some of the dirty work since this is going to get complicated. Your paperwork will reflect other taxes as well like the CIF fee (cost, insurance, and freight), consumption tax (starts at 5% of the CIF), sales tax (13%), and the oddly named Tax Law No. 6946 (1% tax on the CIF price). Are you still with me?

What you should take from this chapter is that it will cost more than you think, so it's worth carefully planning what you want to ship. If there are things you can do without, sell or donate them.

I think the best part of shipping your things could be having a little piece of home once you get here. Sometimes that can make this transition easier. Your dog, Fido, will have his favorite pillow, and if Fido is happy, everyone else will be happy, too.

Link:

The Costa Rican Customs Department: www.hacienda.go.cr

Barry the Shipper Extraordinaire

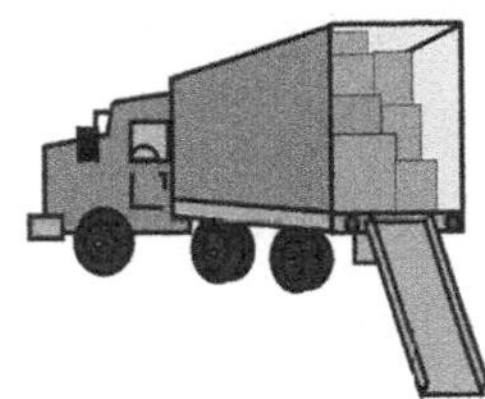

"I want to turn my house upside down and get rid of everything that falls out. Except your father."

~ My Mom

If I could assemble patrons for my own Cheers bar, Barry the shipper would be Norm Peterson. When he entered, everyone would yell out, "Barry," and he'd always sit at the end with a cold beer already waiting for him.

He'd tell Barry-isms about life in Costa Rica and share funny stories about what people have tried to smuggle into the country. Seriously, this guy has a great sense of humor, and you would too if you'd been doing business in Costa Rica for fifteen years.

Barry knows the ins and outs of this process like no one else. When you ask people which shipping company to use, they all say, "Just call Barry." I actually think that should be the name of his business. Because that's precisely what I did when starting this chapter.

I asked him what he would like people to know about shipping their household items to Costa Rica. He murmured a quick, "Hm...," then followed up with, "Well..." and then said, "Let's start from the beginning." This is the exact same response I give when people ask me how long it takes to get residency in Costa Rica.

"There are the large, international moving companies that can haul your stuff anywhere in the world. But that's not the most important part of the equation. It's not the getting it here that's most essential. It's the receiving it that's the crucial part of this endeavor.

"Costa Rica, unlike other countries, has import duties on everything from old socks to blenders. And when that shipping container gets trucked into the receiving warehouse in San José, you better have a broker there who knows what they're doing.

"This is why I don't recommend the big-name companies. Their job is just to get your items to Costa Rica, and customs is a lesser concern for them. It's another reason I don't recommend you doing this on your own unless you fully understand how this process works.

"And one of the most important things you need to consider is that often trucks can't get to your house in Costa Rica. There may be a narrow bridge they can't cross or a left turn that's too sharp. You have to make sure your driver is prepared when that happens."

"So what does your driver do when he can't reach the house?" I asked.

"He'll go back into town and hire a crew. They will then empty the truck, piece by piece, and walk it to the house. Believe me, this happens a lot. And don't get me started on those narrow spiral staircases! Furniture can rarely be carried up those, so we end up having to lift it to the second floor and through sliding glass doors."

When beginning the process of shipping your stuff, one never thinks about the logistics. We figure that every company will have their act in order. "How bad can it be?" my husband would say. But Costa Rica is tricky, and it's important to hire someone that can not only accurately estimate the taxes for your shipment, but get it to your door as well.

Where to Begin

- Decide on a twenty- or forty-foot container. A twenty-foot can fit the contents of a three-bedroom house. The forty-foot can fit the contents of a larger home, and there's usually space for a vehicle.
- Make a thorough list of your items. And I mean everything! Barry is 99%–100% accurate on what your taxes will be.
- Call Barry, and he will arrange for a shipping container to arrive at your house. Make sure you've hired a team to move your items into the shipping container.

- The container will be driven to a port and hauled onto a shipping vessel.
- It arrives at the secure San José customs warehouse.
- Your broker will inspect the container and its contents before moving it onto the delivery truck.

Shipping Your Car: Your car is the last thing to go into the container. It should be backed in and facing out. You can stuff items inside your car, but they must be packed, numbered and put on the inventory list. If you are only shipping a car, you need to check and ask if you can bring more things inside it.

Many shippers do not allow anything in cars. When Barry imports a car, he can pay the taxes, RTV, registration, plates, and stickers and deliver it to the client. Sometimes, if there is enough lead time, he can even have it at the airport when the client arrives.

Don't try to fudge and decrease the value of your car. It's fraud, and it almost always backfires. Barry knows of one case where a clear title was held up for five years. Don't even think about it.

Things Not To Do To Barry

Don't lie and tell Barry your brand-new $25,000 Italian dining room table is from Ikea. Especially when that dining room table is factory-wrapped with the $25,000 price tag attached to it. In Italian.

Don't surprise Barry with forty-eight bags of dog food in the container. That's considered commercial merchandise and will not be taxed at the same rate.

Don't hide weapons in your tackle box. No one likes that.

Just Call Barry!

Email: barry@shipcostarica.com

US Phone: 843-278-5573

Tree Frog

Tax on Commonly Imported Items

Acoustic guitar — 29.95%
Automotive body parts — 42.78%
Bicycle worth more than $1000 — 29.95%
Bicycle worth less than $1000 — 13.00%
Blender — 49.25%
Camera — 13.00%
Camera lens, tripod, accessories — 14.13%
Carpet — 29.93%
Ceramic plates — 29.95%
Clothing — 29.95%
Coffeemaker — 49.27%
Computer (laptop or desktop) — 13.00%
Copy machine — 14.13%
Drinking glass — 29.95%
Drum and drum set — 24.30%
DVD player — 49.27%
Electric guitar — 24.30%

Faucets — 29.95%
Fishing reel — 14.13%
Fishing rod — 24.30%
Furniture — 29.95%
Golf clubs or golf balls — 24.30%
Hair dryer — 49.27%
Home appliances — 49.27%
Hose — 19.78%
Jewelry — 29.95%
Lamp — 29.95%
Mattress — 29.95%
Microwave — 37.58%
Mixer — 49.27%
Musical keyboard — 24.30%
Pots and pans — 29.95%
Printer — 13.00%
Refrigerator — 81.48%
Sewing machine — 14.13%
Sheets — 29.95%
Shoes — 29.95%
Soccer ball — 24.30%
Stringed musical instruments — 30.00%
Television — 49.27%
Tools — 14.13%
Towels — 29.95%
Toy — 29.95%
Umbrella — 29.95%
Vacuum cleaner — 49.27%
Video camera — 14.13%
Video game — 55.55%

Water filter — 14.13%

Water pump — 14.13%

Weapons — 30.00%

Weigh scale — 14.13%

Woodwind musical instrument — 24.30%

Link:

The Costa Rican Customs Department (Dirección General de Aduanas) is overseen by the Costa Rican Department of the Treasury (Ministerio de Hacienda):
www.hacienda.go.cr

Pets

"I think I have the right to resent, to object to libelous statements about my dog."

~ Franklin Delano Roosevelt

What about Fido and Bugsy? We can't possibly leave them behind, so let's go through the list on how to get them here.

Unlike other countries, Costa Rica does not have a quarantine policy. You can get take your animals from the airport to your new home right away.

Certain requirements must be met, so don't skip any of the following steps. You'd be surprised how challenging this process can be if you don't have all your ducks in a row. And if you are bringing a duck, or any other bird, you're not allowed to export them back out of the country. So Costa Rica is their final destination.

Pet Checklist

- ☐ An international certificate from your veterinarian (Form 7001), stating that the animals have had the proper shots. Your veterinarian should be familiar with the necessary forms. The paperwork should be prepared within 14 days of your departure date. You will need duplicates since you will be handing one of these to customs. Your pet must be vaccinated more than 21 days prior to entering the country. Cats and dogs must enter the country at least 30 days before the expiration of the rabies vaccine.
- ☐ Dogs require the following shots: distemper, hepatitis, leptospirosis, parvovirus and rabies vaccinations. Cats require vaccinations against panleukopenia, feline leukemia, feline viral rhinotracheitis, and rabies. (Note: Costa Rica does not honor the three-year rabies vaccination.)
- ☐ Customs will require a market value for your pet. Anything under one hundred dollars is considered noncommercial. Anything over that amount may result in you paying tax.
- ☐ These papers will then need to be endorsed by your state's US Department of Agriculture office (CFIA if you're from Canada). It will cost approximately $45. Many times this office can be found in your state's capital. I went there in person to do it. If you can't do that, make sure you get the package there and back in the allotted amount of time.
- ☐ Make four copies of all paperwork. Also, have copies of your passport handy.

- ☐ Be aware that each airline has its own rules regarding transporting animals. Check with them before booking your trip to ensure you have the proper paperwork.

Even if you're just bringing your pet into the country for a short vacation, you must follow the same process. You will be able to return to the US with no additional paperwork as long as your trip concludes within the timeframe of your Certificate of Health.

When to Fly?

You should fly your pet at times of the year when the weather isn't too hot or too cold. This may completely change the timing of your move. I know it did for me.

Out of all the elements that your pet will be subjected to, heat is the most dangerous. Other factors that may affect your departure date will include how many other passengers are shipping their pets through that airline. Some airlines have guidelines that only allow one animal in the cabin at a time. Since my cat was small enough to fit under my seat, the airline kept delaying my flight to accommodate him. Moving to Costa Rica was one of the biggest decisions of my life, and my cat dictated when I would do it. Isn't that just like a cat?

Crate Size

Airlines are sticklers for the crate size for your animal. The crate must meet IATA (the International Air Transport Association) requirements. Your pet must be able to stand up and turn around. The airline will not allow a pet to fly if it does not have adequate room. This is how a dog that you believed would be traveling as baggage turns out to be traveling as cargo. This occurs when the crate needs to be bigger than you ever anticipated. The only difference between these two is how your pet is processed and what you will be charged for its flight.

The crate must be constructed of sturdy plastic and have adequate ventilation on all four sides, with water and food bowls attached to its door and a copy of the health certificate taped to the top. The lock must be a spring mechanism. It's a good idea to attach a battery-operated fan to your animal's crate, although this isn't required by the airline.

Inside the Cabin vs Baggage vs Cargo

Here's the hiccup: every airline is different, and they may tell you different information each time you contact them. It's frustrating and makes this process even more challenging. Before booking any tickets, call each airline and gather as much information as you can about their pet policy.

If they allow small animals that fit under your seat in the cabin, you're in luck. They will fly with you and you can walk off the plane with them. That's how I got my cat here. If you own a medium-sized dog that fits into a medium-sized pet carrier, it will be considered baggage.

But what if you own a larger breed? Most airlines define this as any dog over seventy pounds. That animal will be considered cargo and will be flown as such.

If you fly into San José, your pooch is sent to the customs warehouse, where an import permit from the Animal Quarantine Offices (SENASA- de Dirección Cuarentena Animal) is required. The cost is roughly $20. There may be other fees as well. My girlfriend Sandy paid $200 to get her dog out of "doggy customs jail."

Unaccompanied Pets

If the pets are unaccompanied, they're automatically considered cargo, and you will need to hire a pet specialist or broker. They'll take care of everything at the customs warehouse.

The Liberia airport does not yet have a customs warehouse, so your pets are brought to the baggage area. It's why many people will fly their pets designated as cargo into the Liberia airport and drive the rest of the way to their location. I would recommend doing this if you are concerned about your pets ending up in the "doggy slammer" in San José.

Links:

USDA APIS Pet Travel: www.aphis.usda.gov/aphis/pet-travel/by-country/pettravel-costa-rica

National Animal Health Service: www.senasa.go.cr/

Airports: San José vs Liberia

"I would rather own a little and see the world than own the world and see a little."
~ Alexander Sattler

There are two international airports. Commonly referred to as the **San José Airport**, the Juan Santamaría International Airport (SJO) is the less expensive of the two and is located in the center of the country. It's bigger and busier than the Liberia airport, and a Hampton Inn Express and Denny's restaurant are located directly across the street. This airport is located three hours from Arenal, two hours from Jacó, and about four hours from Tamarindo. I would fly into this airport if your itinerary takes you down the southern Pacific highway to hot spots like Manuel Antonio, Dominical, or the Osa Peninsula.

Liberia's Daniel Oduber International Airport (LIR) is located in the northwest, Guanacaste region. There is a Hilton Garden Hotel right across the street if you need a nearby place to spend the night. It's a thirty-five-minute drive to Playa del Coco, an hour to Brasilito and Flamingo, an hour and fifteen minutes to Tamarindo, two hours to Samara, and three hours to Arenal. If you're looking for a fabulous beach vacation on the Gold Coast, this is the way to go.

It's a much smaller airport than San José, and as I mentioned in the pet chapter, it's where many people fly in with their pets. It also has a small quirk.

Weird Fact: Your plane may not taxi to a gate at Liberia Airport but may stop on the tarmac instead. Keep this in mind, and let the flight attendants know ahead of time if you will require assistance. They're always helpful. The first time I did this, I felt like Mick Jagger exiting my private jet.

Baggage Carousel

If the baggage carousel is overcrowded with suitcases, a worker will start taking them off and putting them aside to make room. Many times people are frantically looking for their luggage only to find it's standing alongside a dozen others in a corner. If you see a lot of luggage stacked together, don't assume it's for a group of travelers. Go over and start looking through the pieces for yours.

Oversized bags are unloaded in another location. If you can't find this area, ask the guy walking past with his surfboard. He'll be friendly. Most surfers are.

Immigration

At immigration, you will hand the attendant your passport and the form you filled out on the plane. Make sure you fill in your destination!

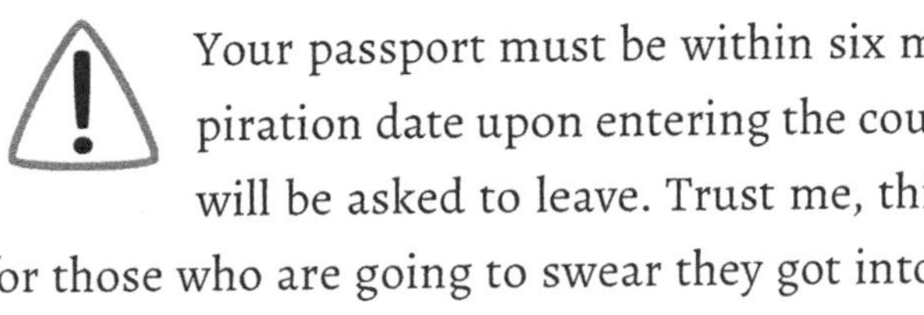

Your passport must be within six months of its expiration date upon entering the country. If not, you will be asked to leave. Trust me, this happens. And for those who are going to swear they got into the country on a passport expiring sooner, I believe you. You don't have to go into the Facebook forums and tell them I'm clueless. I already know that. Remember: when in Costa Rica results may vary.

Customs

Customs is an easy process if you don't have too many bags. If you do, they may pull you aside to see if you're bringing in commercial items for resale.

Before packing, remove all price tags from your clothing. If you leave the price tags on, it may appear as if you're planning to resell the garment. Also, take new items out of their original packaging.

Departing the Country and Exit Tax

When returning to the airport for your flight home, you may or may not have to pay the $29 per person exit tax. Many airlines are finally phasing this out and including it in their ticket price. **I found it on my United airline ticket listed as:**

International Boarding tax—$27 and Costa Rica Baggage Inspection Fee—$2.

If you need to pay this exit tax, there is a special window for this. Be sure to pay this tax before getting in line for your boarding pass. After paying the exit tax, you will receive a form similar to the immigration one you had previously filled out on the plane during your inbound flight to Costa Rica. Turn the exit tax receipt over, grab a pen, and fill this out before queuing up in front of the airline counter. The last time I did this, the print was so small I needed the Hubble Telescope to read it. I have to find who is in charge of the font division in making their forms. Probably a guy named Chuck who's going through a contentious divorce. He wants everyone to suffer.

This tax can be paid in advance at the Bank of Costa Rica, but it's actually quicker to do it at the airport. But make sure you didn't already pay this as part of your airline ticket. You don't want to end up paying twice. It's better to pay with cash or a debit card. If you pay with a credit card, it's considered a cash advance, and you may receive a charge on your credit card statement (mine was ten dollars).

Now that you've gone through immigration, retrieved your bags, and made it through customs, how will you get to your resort? Navigating the tricky maze of taxis, gypsy cabs, shuttle buses, and rental cars without losing your mind is an art unto itself. In the next chapter, we'll discuss how to get you to that beachside hammock in no time.

- Liberia airport food is expensive—really expensive. So please don't yell out loud when you pay seven dollars for a bottle of water. It's unnerving.
- It's illegal to remove sand or shells from the beaches. They will confiscate them from your suitcase at the airport.
- The currency exchange booth at the airport does not give the best rates.

Links:

Liberia Airport: http://www.liberiacostaricaairport.net/
San José Airport: http://sjoairport.com/en/
Hampton Inn Express Hotel: https://hamptoninn3.hilton.com
Hilton Garden Inn: http://hiltongardeninn3.hilton.com/en/hotels/costa-rica/hilton-garden-inn-liberia-airport-SJOLAGI/index.html

Coatimundi

Transportation

"At the end of your day your feet should be dirty, hair messy, and eyes sparkling."
~ Shanti

You're finally in Costa Rica and starting your family vacation! You're a little nervous because everything is in Spanish, and you're not sure where you're going. Don't be anxious; this is part of the adventure. And even if it's confusing, isn't standing in a Costa Rican airport still better than another day at the office?

Before we tackle the taxi mob, let's talk about buses, private shuttles, and renting a car.

Bus Transportation

If you are a backpacker or just a bargain-lover, there's a public bus stop outside the San José airport. Walk out of the airport and cross the street. Make a left and follow the sidewalk around the parking garage. Once at the street, look to your right, and you'll see a bus stop approximately seventy feet away. There will be a gas station across from the bus stop. From here, you will most likely be going straight to the bus terminal in San José because almost all routes around the country start there. Be aware that there are a few bus stations in San José, and not all of them will offer routes to your final destination.

The Liberia airport's bus stop is at the entrance of the airport which is about a mile away from the terminal. Bring water if walking to it. It gets hot in Guanacaste.

The Facebook group Costa Rica By Bus and the app Off the Grid Traveler are great resources for navigating tricky Costa Rican bus schedules.

It's a good idea to know some Spanish, because the bus driver will most likely not understand English. Make sure to ask where the bus you're boarding is headed. Although the sign may say San José, the driver may have forgotten to update it, and your bus may actually be going in the opposite direction.

Always be aware of your bag on a bus. Thieves love it when you place it in the overhead bin. It's easy for them to snatch it and run. This is where a PacSafe bag would be great. If your bag is too big and the driver wants to place it underneath the bus, pay for a second seat and place it there.

Private Shuttles

If public transportation isn't for you, there are also private shuttle buses. Interbus is one company that services a large variety of locations, such as Playa Hermosa, Tamarindo, Flamingo, Conchal, Samara, Monteverde, La Fortuna, Jacó, Manuel Antonio, and Puerto Viejo. They may even drop you off at your hotel. It's a safe option, but wait time can be extensive. These buses are often expecting passengers coming into the country on many different flights. Your bus will not depart until all of its customers have arrived. The good news is you can see these buses throughout the country, and they always appear to be clean and air-conditioned.

I recently found a great option if you plan on landing at the Liberia airport. Tamarindo Transfers & Tours (aka Tamarindo Shuttle) is widely known for offering the most competitive rates for an airport shuttle from Tamarindo to the Liberia airport. Their vehicles are clean and air-conditioned. Depending on their schedule, they will also drop you off at other locations in the Tamarindo area. They're nice and helpful, so call before you arrive to see if they can accommodate your needs.

Renting a Car

If you're planning on renting a car at either airport, rental agencies have shuttles available that will take you directly to their offices. Most agencies are only a few miles away from the airport. I enjoy renting a car since I like to travel on my own schedule, and the best things are often off the beaten path. Read my chapter "Renting a Car" for more information.

Uber

Uber's legality is questionable in Costa Rica. Although Uber is available in San José and throughout the Central Valley, there is considerable hostility between them and licensed taxi drivers.

Taxi

If you're not using any of the options above, perhaps a taxi will work best for you. Let's try to break down the taxi system in Costa Rica. It's going to be tricky, but if you follow some basic rules, you should be fine.

As in most countries, there can be unlicensed gypsy cab drivers waiting at the airport. They will approach you and try to steer you toward their cabs. You should avoid this. It is more important to get safely to your destination than to haggle for the cheapest fare. I'm not saying gypsy cab drivers are bad people. Most are just trying to make a living, but without a license there is no way to know the intentions of your driver.

A licensed taxi driver should be wearing a blue badge, dark brown pants, and a white shirt. Many drivers will approach you, so be prepared! They'll be driving orange cars and working off their meters (*la maria*). All public drivers are registered with a special code that can be found on the dashboard. You should write this number down. If you forget anything in the cab, or have a problem, you will be able to identify the vehicle you were riding in. The driver should not be asking for personal information. Do not give your passport number to any taxi driver. There are reasons your hotel may need this information, but not your cab driver.

I have had many experiences with taxi drivers. Some were good and some were bad. But you can limit your risk by following the rules above.

If you would rather not drive or deal with a taxi, there is another option: a personal driver. And I have just the guys for you.

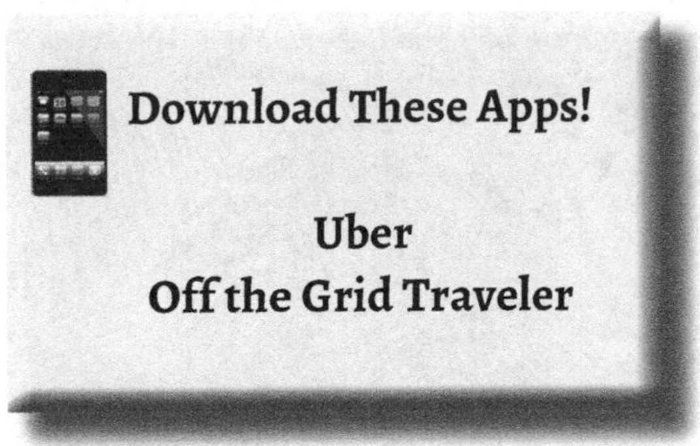

Download These Apps!
Uber
Off the Grid Traveler

Links:

Costa Rica By Bus:

www.facebook.com/groups/CostaRicaByBus

https://costaricabybus.wordpress.com

Interbus: www.interbusonline.com

Tamarindo Transfers & Tours: www.tamarindoshuttle.com

- Shuttle Reservations: (506) 2653-4444
- Or in the US at (848) 480-6096

Sunrise, Osa Peninsula

Daniel: Your San José Personal Driver

"One of the great things about travel is you find out how many good, kind people there are."

~ Edith Wharton

Ticos love their country, and if you get to spend time with them, they'll share little bits of secret information with you: tiny gems that will make you wonder if you can ever leave this beautiful place.

"That hot spring is nice, but go down the road a couple of kilometers and make a left. It's free there, and it's the prettiest spot in the entire area," a Tico will tell me. Or, "This place is beautiful, but walk around the rocks to the adjacent cove, and you will find a deserted beach with tiny pink shells scattered across the sand."

Daniel is that Tico. He is a taxi and private driver in San José who was hired by one of my readers. I'm so lucky to have met him. He is incredibly helpful, translating for them, finding the best restaurants, and making sure they're well taken care of. But most importantly, Daniel is just a nice guy doing a great job.

What I love about Daniel is that he'll take you not only to all the touristy places but also to the in-the-know spots. And these are the places that turn a trip into an adventure. It's seeing a country from the inside out, in a way that's impossible if you're staying at an all-inclusive resort for a week.

I recently asked Daniel what the typical itinerary is, and he was more than excited to answer.

"That would depend on the area my clients want to go. But if someone said, 'I have no plans, surprise me!' I start with a trip to the central Pacific.

"We make a quick stop in Caldera to experience some capuchin monkeys in the wild. And these monkeys are very funny and mischievous; they come down from the trees and try to steal whatever is in your backpack. They love anything shiny.

"We'll stop in Puntarenas in the Paseo de los Turistas for lunch. I know good places that serve awesome food and seafood at Tico prices. I'll suggest a Churchill for dessert (similar to a snow cone but with fruit, condensed milk, powdered milk, and flavored syrup) while waiting for the ferry boat to go across the Peninsula de Nicoya.

"At the other side, there will be plenty of choices and breathtaking places at which you don't have to pay an entrance fee to visit. Places like Playa Blanca, Montezuma Beach, or interesting things like Cabuya Island Cemetery. It's a beautiful island you can walk out to at low tide and snorkel.

"We'll stop at Cabo Blanco Nature Reserve, the oldest reserve in Costa Rica. It's a seabird sanctuary and provides refuge to an abundance of animals: coatis, capuchin monkeys, coyotes, deer, and anteaters.

"I also love to introduce my clients to the beaches of Santa Teresa and Mal País, explore the local landscapes and waterfalls, and share with them the folklore and traditions of the area. This is my country, and I love every corner of it."

Daniel stated that he is saving for a shuttle bus. It's a lofty goal since cars are extremely expensive in Costa Rica, but he has dreams of one day expanding his business and providing more services. I know he will get there because he gives his clients a safe, fun, and unique Costa Rican adventure.

You'll realize that after hiring Daniel, he quickly becomes your friend, and eating a snow cone with your pal while waiting for a ferry sounds like the best kind of trip.

Daniel Campos

www.facebook.com/TrueDriverCostaRica

Email: yoamocostarica@gmail.com

Toucan

"

Dervin: Your Liberia Personal Driver

"Travelling is like flirting with life. It's like saying, 'I would stay and love you, but I have to go; this is my station.'"

~ Lisa St. Aubin de Teran

The Guanacaste coast is a fun-filled playground. Whether it's kayaking, stand-up paddleboarding, horseback riding, or ATV-ing, you'll want to squeeze in as much as possible. My friend and tour guide Dervin Suarez is the Tico that can make this happen. He can pick you up at Liberia Airport in the morning, have you flying high along a zip line that afternoon, and ensure you'll have wonderful memories during your time in his country.

Dervin was born in Guanacaste and graduated college with a business degree that had an emphasis in tourism. He has since worked in all areas of tourism, from sportfishing to butterfly farms. There is not one question he cannot answer about Costa Rica.

So what are your plans? Thinking about kayaking? He'll have you snorkeling and eating fruit at Isla Plata off Playa Flamingo. You'll want this day to last forever.

How about fishing? Sportfishing is one of the more popular excursions, and depending on the time of the year, you may catch tuna, mahi-mahi, red snapper, or even a marlin! Maybe you'll want to try your hand at surfing. He has the best instructors and knows one particular spot where the break is perfect for beginners.

Do you want to visit a volcano? Dervin can arrange a day trip to the majestic Arenal Volcano, where you can hike through the national park, walk across hanging bridges, and end the day relaxing in natural hot springs. You can't do that in Cincinnati, folks!

My friend can show you all of these things, but there's one place he takes his clients that's even more special, a spot where you'll truly understand why so many people fall in love with this country.

"To see some of the most beautiful wildlife," he says, "I take my clients on a riverboat tour down the Tempisque River. It's here you'll see iguanas, howler and white-faced monkeys, crocodiles, and many aquatic birds like herons and egrets. If we go during mango season, we'll even see scarlet macaws nesting. What a wonderful sight! If you're a bird lover, this is an incredible experience you won't want to miss.

"After the riverboat tour, we go to a farm where the owners cook an authentic Costa Rican meal over a wood fire: corn tortillas, smoked cheese, sweet plantains, beans, rice, pollo en salsa, rice pudding, and of course, fresh coffee.

"Have you ever tried vino de coyol? It comes from the sap of the coyol palm. After the palm is cut down, they collect the fermenting sap. You'll see this sold on the side of the road everywhere in Costa Rica.

"Children love the domestic animals on the farm: horses, cows, baby goats, and chickens. It's a beautiful piece of land surrounded by mango trees. The farmhouse has antique tools, and you'll see how Costa Ricans lived years ago, when there were no roads and the only way to transport sugar cane to Puntenares was by ferryboat.

"This adventure is approximately 6 1/2 hours. Whether you're a bird watcher, animal lover, or foodie, this tour has something for every member of your family. It's truly an authentic Costa Rica experience, a glimpse of life in my country and why it's one of the most special places on earth."

After the zip-lining and beach hopping, I wouldn't hesitate to go on Dervin's special tour for an authentic taste of Costa Rica.

Dervin Suarez
Sportfishing: www.yellowfinsportfishing.com
Tours: www.yellowfinguanacaste.com
Email: yellowfin@racsa.co.cr

Morpho Butterfly

Renting a Car

"I am not the same having seen the moon shine on the other side of the world."

~ Mary Anne Radmacher Hershey

You made it! You gathered your luggage, walked through customs, and are ready to begin your Costa Rica adventure. You've decided to rent a car because you plan on exploring this beautiful country. And trust me, there is a lot to explore.

Costa Rica is spread out. She has miles of beautiful beaches, some nestled in coves within five minutes from one another. Having a car means you can beach hop all day, or you can take off in the morning to tour that animal sanctuary before ziplining with the kids in the afternoon. Being mobile means you can fit a whole lot more into your schedule.

Some people may be hesitant about renting a car. I understand their reservations, but with navigational apps, it's easier than ever now to get to the top of a volcano in the morning and the beach by the afternoon.

I've hosted many people at The Happier House who have rented from different rental agencies. The business that gets the most praise is Vamos Rent-A-Car. They're friendly from the moment you walk into their office, and they take the time to answer your questions. But most importantly, there are no surprises with the price. My guests arrive happy and ready to begin their fabulous vacation.

Unfortunately, I've also had guests that were quoted a price of $7 per day (from other rental car agencies) on third-party sites, and when they got to the rental counter, it turned out the cost was ten times more. Understandably, this starts a vacation off on the wrong foot. It stinks when I see this happen. So to figure out how to avoid this, I reached out to Alex Villalobos, operations manager at Vamos Rent-A-Car (vamosrentacar.com). He was gracious and willing to shed some of that golden Costa Rican light on this topic.

What are the insurance fees? I understand one is mandatory in Costa Rica.

"This is a very good question. There are two related costs associated with insurance needs for Costa Rica. The first is a governmental requirement, similar to Ireland, Italy, and Mexico, called Third Party Liability (TPL), also referred to as SLI, or the frequently used term Mandatory Insurance. The cost for this waiver typically varies between $12 and $25 per day based on the car category—e.g., sedan or full-size SUV—and individual rental agency.

"The second requirement is a Collision Damage Waiver, or CDW. This may come in two forms, either through the use of a credit card provider's perk or from purchasing in-house coverage from the rental provider. In the first case, the renter should bring a personalized letter from said credit card provider that includes their name, the last four digits of their credit card number, and the amount of coverage provided, and specifically states that car rental in Costa Rica is part of their coverage plan. However, this is not the only concern with using a credit card program. Many have additional stipulations regarding the covered vehicle and its usage, such as the number of passengers (generally more than seven and the rental is not covered), and the road conditions, as many have an 'off-road' clause, which Costa Rica technically falls into on many cases.

"We advise to check directly with the policy provider to get exact details. If there is a claim or accident, the renter is responsible for the repair damages upfront; you must communicate with your credit card company personally for reimbursement."

Are there other fees I should know about?

"Renters should be aware that car rental agencies with a desk inside the airport building normally charge what is called an 'airport tax' (which can be as much as 14% extra) to balance the cost of renting and manning the desk, even though this is not a legally mandated tax. The same can be said for 'environmental' and 'license plate' fees. These are hidden costs used to pad the advertised lower rates.

"Other fees may be incurred for extra services such as additional drivers, cooler, GPS system, child seating, a Wi-Fi hotspot, and roof racks, many of which rent at a daily rate. Furthermore, delivery or a return location differing from the pickup location will result in additional charges, as will opening the office beyond normal business hours.

"To receive an accurate quote, we recommend contacting the local branch, using their country-specific website to see the proper insurance and fees. Calling them to double-check is also useful, as is doing business with well-established companies that have good reviews on trustworthy websites such as TripAdvisor.com."

Some sites quote a car for $7/ day, and it shocks people when they find out that's not accurate. I notice you do not do this.

"Some agencies and third-party websites such as Expedia, Kayak, and other portal websites will advertise daily car rental rates at prices that are so low they would be unprofitable. If the SLI cost (the Mandatory Insurance) is over $12, then the only way in which a car rental agency can rent a vehicle for $7 is to pay the client to rent the car! It does not make sense.

"It is a very competitive market. This leads to unrealistic pricing being promoted to draw in unsuspecting renters. Once you're standing at the counter, bags in hand and tired from the flight, you're more likely to break down and pay it than walk out. This inevitably leads to very unhappy and angry customers.

"At Vamos, our commitment to no hidden fees and transparent pricing is driven by our belief that happy, satisfied customers are the best clients! Word of mouth has built our business; we strive daily to be worthy of that praise."

When purchasing full insurance, are all potential damages covered?

"To preface this question, we should discuss negligence. While some companies may differ on the definition, Vamos explains several ways to void the Collision Damage Waiver (CDW), thus holding the renter 100% responsible for all damages, on our website, but the simple answer is 'by doing things that one should not do in the first place if common sense were used.'

"Now, with that aside, a typical tourist with Full CDW would only be held responsible for damages to the sound system, roof rack, underside or interior of the vehicle, except in cases of collisions or theft of vehicle where they are exempt. Furthermore, tow truck service or vehicle recovery, in the case of an accident or overturning of the vehicle, are not included."

Under what specific circumstances will damages be considered negligence and not be covered?

"Per our website, we list the circumstances where insurance would be voided as:

- The driver is not authorized by Vamos Rent-A-Car to operate the vehicle.
- The driver is under the influence of alcohol and/or illegal substances.

- The driver operates the vehicle contrary to the laws of Costa Rica.
- The driver does not provide an accident report from the local authorities.
- The vehicle undergoes misuse or negligence, such as, but not limited to: driving with the parking brake on, operating the transmission in 4x4 mode over 40 km/h, hitting obstacles on the road, driving on roads in poor condition and/or driving in, through or over rivers, estuaries and/or beaches.

"There may be legal roads that pass through rivers. However, these should only be crossed during dry season when the water level is below tire level or when the riverbed is dry. Otherwise, the driver must find a different route or park in a secure lot and walk. When in doubt, get out and measure the water with a stick or your foot to see how deep it is before entering with the vehicle.

"**Driving on beaches is against the law**, so that would void our waiver and could incur a traffic fine. Sand wrecks a vehicle from the wheel bearings to brakes to air filters and is abrasive to paintwork and the windshield. Tidal waters pose a grave danger to vehicles parked on the beach as a further deterrent."

What is a temporary hold on your credit card? Is that a deposit?

"Since vehicles in Costa Rica are more expensive than in most other industrialized countries due to the high import tariffs, the rental agencies need a form of protection on their investment. Besides acting as security, the hold is used as payment if the need arises.

"For example, for a minor fender bender where the damage is minimal (say under $200), the hold would be reduced by the amount of the damages. At the end of the rental period, the renter would receive the remainder, after their credit card company processes the international charge. This typically takes two to five business days.

"At Vamos, we have three different deposit amounts, all depending on the insurance waiver selected. If a renter chooses to forego our in-house CDWs by using an approved credit card program, then the deposit is $2,000. If this amount eats into too much of the available credit limit, or if the renter does not have this perk from their credit card provider since the total rental fee is also held, renters may opt for either the Basic CDW ($750 deposit) or the Full CDW ($100 deposit) option.

"Although not a transaction per se, the hold will reduce the amount of the available credit limit on the card. We advise renters to bring a backup credit card for purchases during the vacation so as not to max out the rental card."

Does Vamos have offices around the country in case I break down?

"Vamos has offices near the airports in Liberia and San José, but we offer nationwide road assistance from mechanics sent from the nearest office or through our network of garages and mechanics across Costa Rica. Whether we fix or exchange the vehicle, our aim is to get our clients back on the road as quickly as possible."

And lastly, what would you like travelers to remember about Costa Rica?

"The pride I feel for Costa Rica comes from our commitment to nature and the Ticos. Regarding the environment, there's still room for improvement, but in many ways, we're leading the way. Twenty-seven percent of all Costa Rican land is protected, saving rainforests and animals for the future generations. Our power needs are being met by renewable sources with the goal to be carbon-neutral by 2021.

"We have the largest hydropower plant in Central America, producing 305.5 MW, and it's also the second largest infrastructure right after the Panama Canal. Here's a bit of history that's stuck with me: Costa Rica's first electric power plant was also hydro powered, back in 1884. Parts were imported from Thompson-Houston Company in Massachusetts to capture a waterfall's energy to water oxen. All of this was planned by Ticos. Costa Rican people have made this country what it is today.

"Tico society is very family-oriented and warm. People are patriotic and keen to show the best of their country to visitors. They are Pura Vida. While traveling in Costa Rica, it's easy to see that people are smiling, willing to help and make it feel like home."

Alex's Checklist & Tips for Renting a Car

- ☐ Use the local, country-specific website (not the corporate headquarters') to price check or reserve the vehicle.
- ☐ Ask about the quote:
    a. Is the "mandatory insurance" included?

b. Will there be any additional fees once I arrive?
c. Can I decline their CDW and use my own credit card company's program?

- ☐ Check the arrival time and when the car rental office opens. Early or late flights may play a part in your decision.
- ☐ Ask what types of payment and credit cards are accepted.
- ☐ Do they accept non-raised lettering on credit cards? For some reason, all the old card imprint machines have found their way to Costa Rica, and some smaller firms do not take the newer, "flat" credit cards.
- ☐ Check age requirements. Company policy differs depending on the agency, but we allow 18- to 20-year-olds to be on the rental agreement with the stipulation that only the Basic CDW is available and its deductible is doubled (from $975 to $1950). Twenty-one and older have no additional rules at Vamos.
- ☐ Inquire if there are any specials or discounts.
- ☐ Do they allow pets?
- ☐ Are there any out-of-the-ordinary service fees like an excessively dirty car fee?

General Tips:

- Carry a few dollars' worth of Costa Rican currency for tolls.
- Don't leave valuables in the rental car.
- Don't bribe police officers, and report any official who asks for a bribe.
- Don't move your vehicle after an accident unless directed to do so by an authority, nor should you ever leave the

scene before the police and an insurance representative arrive.

Links:

Vamos Rent-A-Car

www.vamosrentacar.com

FAQ page: www.vamosrentacar.com/faq

~This is an excellent source for information, don't skip it

Blog posts: driving tips

www.vamosrentacar.com/driving-tips-costa-rica

Zip-lining Video: https://youtu.be/Xf2NfB4w5fY

GPS, Directions & Mango Trees

"Not all those who wander are lost."
~ J.R.R. Tolkien

Two hundred meters past the mango tree. That's what you'll hear when asking for directions in Costa Rica. Before I moved to Costa Rica, I never saw a mango tree in my life. And what is two hundred meters, anyway? How do I judge that? The good news is you'll soon be able to identify a mango tree, and you'll swiftly abandon any benchmark of what a conventional postal system looks like.

There are no conventional addresses in Costa Rica so be prepared.

Some of the best adventures Rob and I had were when we got lost. We've found amazing beaches, incredible people, and crazy Chihuahuas all because we ventured down an unmarked road. And then there was the time we almost drove off a mountain, but that was because we were looking for pizza.

A typical block is 100 meters.

Luckily, most everyone has a cell phone and can use it to download all sorts of navigational apps, like Waze and Google Maps. They've even replaced dashboard GPS devices, but many rental car agencies will still provide these for a fee. Navigating these numerous mango trees has never been easier, and you're likely to get where you're going... likely. This is the dilemma you'll eventually encounter: GPS will suggest a route. By all accounts, it looks like a fine thoroughfare.

"Maybe we'll get lucky, and it'll be a scenic tour throughout the countryside," Jim will say to Hazel.

And Jim is right. It will be scenic. Four hours of scenic views from a potholed dirt road that leaves Hazel mildly concussed. So to avoid this, have a paper map and GPS.

It's very common for expats to recommend alternate routes from what your GPS suggests. This is because we know about a river that may be impassable in the rainy season, or a dirt road that hasn't been graded in a year, or a tree that has fallen and blocked the street. This is the regular kind of chitchat down here.

Waze is an excellent app that will alert you to traffic jams, police checkpoints, and accidents. I find that more and more people are using Waze in Costa Rica, so it's constantly updated with input from thousands of drivers.

With these above apps and a paper map, you should never have to worry about getting lost in Costa Rica. Okay, maybe you'll get a little lost, but you'll eventually make it to your destination.

It's always two hundred meters past the mango tree.

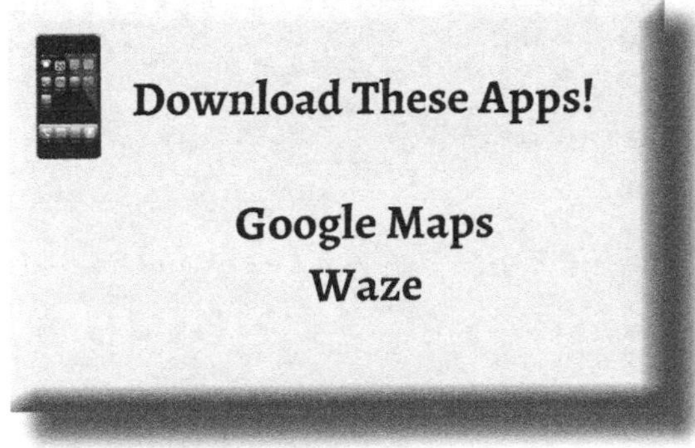
Download These Apps!
Google Maps
Waze

Guanacaste
Hummingbird
Golden-hooded
Tanager

Monkey Money

"Money often costs too much."
~ Ralph Waldo Emerson

Costa Rica has pretty money. In comparison, the United States' currency is that girl at the prom with a bad perm. Costa Rica's currency, colones (₡), is Grace Kelly... at the Oscars. There are monkeys, butterflies, sloths, and hummingbirds on their bills. It's a small thing that always makes me smile.

What doesn't make me smile is that this money is confusing. The ATM will spit out a 10,000 colones bill, and you're already booking a private jet to the Riviera. But hold on there, big spender: you are not rich. That 10,000 colones bill is roughly $20. So here is a phrase you should remember:

Take off three zeros, multiply by two, and subtract 12%.

Let's repeat that. Take off three zeros and multiply by two. That's roughly what your money will be worth in dollars.

(The American dollar is now worth 568 colones.) You will notice that many things are priced in American dollars in Costa Rica. The "take off three zeros and multiply by two" rule is a general idea of what things cost. If you want to be more accurate, use this rule and subtract 12%.

Paper Currency

₡ 1000 (roughly $2 but as of this writing is $1.76)

₡ 5000 (roughly $10 but as of this writing is $8.80)

₡ 10,000 (roughly $20 but as of this writing is $17.60)

₡ 20,000 (roughly $40 but as of this writing is $35.20)

₡ 50,000 (roughly $100 but as of this writing is $88.00)

Coin Currency

There's a different formula for coins (which are not pretty at all): take the value of a coin and divide by five. You will also have to subtract 12% for more accuracy, but this is not a math class, and I can already see you dozing off and wondering when I'm going to start writing about monkeys.

5 colones = 1 cent	50 colones = 10 cents
10 colones = 2 cents	100 colones = 20 cents
25 colones = 5 cents	500 colones = 88 cents

500 Colón Coin: Keep an eye out for the 500 colón coin. Although slightly larger, it looks like the rest of your change, but it is worth roughly eighty-eight cents. Many businesses will consider this coin a dollar when giving back your change. So decide whether you want to argue for that twelve cents they just gypped you or move on with your life.

ATMS

It's very easy to use bank machines in Costa Rica, and you'll often be given a choice of dollars or colones. Just check with your bank to see what kind of fees will be deducted. Often, there is a minimal charge of 3% to perform an international transaction. However, it's nice to avoid waiting in line at a bank to exchange money, and the independent booths at the airport usually don't give the best rates, anyway. So feel confident that your credit and ATM cards might be all you need when traveling throughout the country as a tourist.

Before traveling overseas, contact your bank and credit card companies and notify them about your planned trip. This will prevent them from denying an international transaction for fear the card was stolen. Don't bring ripped or old money. It's very hard to spend that here. Also, many places will not take one hundred or fifty-dollar bills, but you can exchange them at the banks.

Weird Facts: In Costa Rica, the comma in written numbers is a period. For example, 56,800.00 is written as 56.800,00. I call this culture dyslexia.

And as for monkeys, capuchin monkeys will sneak into your backpack and steal your money, car keys, and Doritos.

Now that you understand Costa Rican currency, kindly dog-ear this page in order to make my dad happy. Or if you're reading this on an e-reader, highlight this whole sentence. Whatever you do, please don't stick it in your garage next to that other book about moving to Belize. Keep it in good shape for when you sell it at the flea market for ten cents.

Or price it in Costa Rican currency... fifty colones.

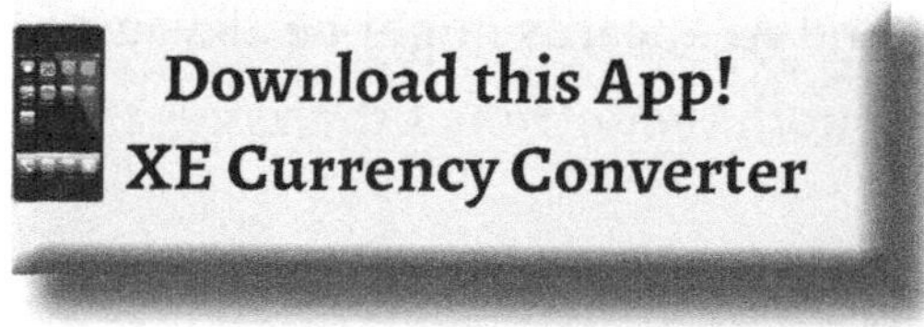
Download this App!
XE Currency Converter

Spreading Roots

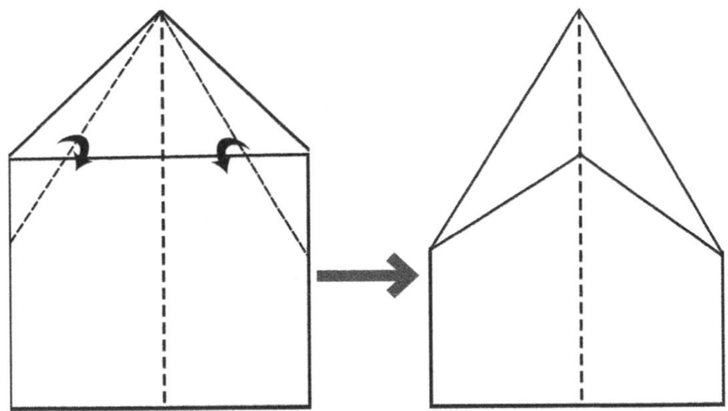

Fold top edges of paper to center line

15 eggs —$2.60

Cabbage—$1 /kg

Loaf of bread—$2.30

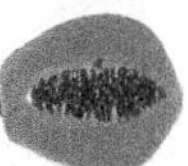
Papaya—$1.25 /kg

Milk (gallon)—$3.30

Zucchini—97¢ each

Stick of butter —$1.54

Celery—$3.20 /kg

Coffee 500 gr—$4.20

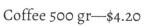

Mushrooms 250 gr
$3.40

Tomato— $1 /kg

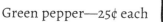

Pasta 250 gr—81¢

Green pepper—25¢ each

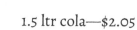

Canned tomato 400 gr
$1.08

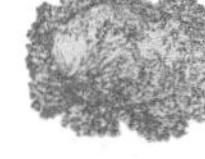
Bag of lettuce 250gr—$2

1.5 ltr cola—$2.05

Broccoli—$2.75 /kg

6 pack beer—$7.25

Carrots—73¢ /kg

Olive oil 500ml
$5.40

Onion—$1.68 /kg

Corn Flakes—$2.75

Watermelon—97¢ /kg

Oreos—$2.73

Pineapple—$1.20 each

Toothpaste—$2.53

Bananas—$1.20 /kg

Chicken Breast—$5 /kg

3 Heads Garlic—55¢

Super Gas—$1.08 /ltr

What's Your Budget?

"A budget takes the fun out of money."
~ Mason Cooley

I received an email from a man named Carl who was moving to Costa Rica with only $500 in savings. "Do you think I can live off that?" he asked.

Since Carl didn't specify a timeframe, my answer was that he could enjoy an amazing day, starting with an ATV tour, followed by a zip-lining excursion, and capping it all off with a sunset catamaran tour.

He could probably stretch that out to a month if he bunked with a few people and stuck to a diet of beans, rice, and produce. But sorry, Carl, you cannot retire in Costa Rica on $500. As Rob's friend Tommy Walnuts would say, "You're wearing short pants, bro." A phrase that my husband had to translate for me since I don't speak Brooklynese.

"It means you're broke," he said. Unfortunately, short pants don't cut it if you're planning on moving to Costa Rica. But you don't need bell bottoms either. I would say capri-length pants are your sweet spot.

One of the major misconceptions is that Costa Rica is extraordinarily inexpensive. The second biggest misconception is that Costa Rica is extraordinarily expensive.

How much does it cost to live in Costa Rica? There is no one answer. Cost of living varies throughout the country and will also depend on how and where you choose to live. Are you willing to share expenses with a roommate? Drive up a mountain road and through a river to a house that's cheaper to rent? Do you eat out often? Do you have children who will need private schooling? Smoke and drink alcohol? Need special medications or have health issues? Or maybe you have a Dorito addiction. Imported goods can cost twice as much in Costa Rica. All of these things play a role when creating your budget.

When we lived in Grecia, our budget was $1000 a month. At the time, it cost about $70 in gas to fill up our SUV, so we often rode our scooter which only cost $6 to fill. And that scooter got us all around the country. In fact, we still have it, and it's one of the first things people comment on when they arrive at The Happier House.

Produce is very affordable, while most animal proteins are expensive (whether in the Central Valley or at the coast). We made low-cost stir-fry meals at home, filling them with more produce than meat. We always shopped at the farmers' market on Saturday, spending $25 there and another $20 at the grocery store. Our rent was $400 a month, and utilities were reasonable: electricity $55, phone $10, internet $30, water $10. Life was good.

When we moved to the beach, our rent was $150 a month, but only because we were house-sitting. Utilities were another story. We started to use much more electricity than when we lived in the mountains. Our electric bill could easily surpass $200 a month due to our need for air conditioning. It gets really hot here, especially during the dry season.

Another big expense when you live at the beach can be water. It's pricey in Guanacaste. If you live in a condominium, your bill could be as low as $10 a month. But if you own a home with a pool and irrigate your landscaping, it can go up into the hundreds.

Groceries are twenty to thirty percent more expensive at the coast. If you buy them at stores near tourist areas, you will pay dearly. Have you ever bought mosquito repellent or sunscreen near a resort? It's like an early 401K penalty.

I'm mindful of where I shop and always look for discounts. On Sundays, chicken is on sale at a local grocery store at $2.55 a pound. It may cost double during the week. On Saturdays, produce is upwards of forty percent off. I didn't have to worry as much about this when I lived in Grecia. It isn't a tourist town, so prices don't vary so widely between stores.

But even at the beach, you can live comfortably for $1500 to $2000 a month. I've seen rents as low as $500 a month and as high as $5000. One has a helicopter pad. And a stable. If that's the lifestyle you're shooting for, kudos to you. Ride off into the sunset while slathering yourself with resort-bought sunscreen.

One thing is for certain: living in the Central Valley is typically more affordable than at the coast. Anytime you're closer to San José, products tend to be cheaper. It's also important not to compare apples to oranges. For an average lifestyle, you might find Costa Rica costs only slightly less than the United States. However, if you're working toward a luxury lifestyle, you may find living at the beach to be much less expensive when compared to living at the beach in the United States. All that being said, what's most important is that you find a place that makes you smile. An area where you wake up in a good mood before your feet even touch the ground.

Rob and I changed many things once we moved to Costa Rica. Some of them were monetary, but most were mental. You can do it too as long as you're flexible, and it's surprising how flexible you become once living a happier life.

So how much does it cost to live in Costa Rica? The short answer is from $500 to $10000 a month. It all depends on whether you're taking your helicopter to the farmers' market or if you're a surfer who plans to live in a van down by the river. For some, being closer to those tasty waves is all they need to be happy.

2.2 pounds = 1 kilogram
1 gallon = 3.78 liters

Link:

YouTube Video: Rob's idea of shopping with our scooter. Wait for the bread...
https://youtu.be/e_CwUfFuzVw

Renting a Home

"Believe you can and you're halfway there."
~ Theodore Roosevelt

What kind of person are you? Do you enjoy the mountains over the beach? Would you rather live in an urban area or in the countryside? Knowing what makes you happy will be the key to finding your happy place.

When we moved, Costa Rica was a lot different than it is today. There was no internet access except for at a café a half hour away. I vividly remember driving down the mountain to email my anxious parents that I hadn't been kidnapped by a pack of monkeys. It was a dial-up connection, which in retrospect would have given monkeys plenty of time to kidnap me.

There was no Skype, Facetime, or high-speed internet. People may argue that there is little high-speed anything in Costa Rica, but I can assure you, we now have internet sufficient to make phone calls, stream videos of goats in pajamas, and share pictures of my life on Facebook. Check out my page; I think you'll love it!

Facebook

Costa Rica has had an explosion of interest over the years, and you'll find many groups on Facebook about living in Costa Rica. There are also forums that list things for sale as well as apartments for rent. I find that this is a great starting point for finding housing.

Airbnb

Airbnb is another good place to begin. Rent short-term with them first, then begin looking for a more permanent housing solution. There are plenty of ways to go about this, but there is one thing for certain:

It's best to have your feet on the ground in Costa Rica first before committing to anything long-term.

Why is that? Because what you see in a picture doesn't always match what you'll see when you get here. Also, do you really want to wire someone you haven't met a large sum of money? I'm sure this has worked out for some people, but to avoid hearing Hazel complain that you rented a house next to a rooster academy, check things out first before putting any money down.

Questions to Ask before Renting

- Can I flush my toilet paper?
- Is cell and internet reception available?
- Who pays utilities?
- Has the house ever been broken into?
- Is the water supply reliable? Is it well or city water?
- What is the monthly water bill? (In Grecia it was negligible; in Guanacaste, it can be $100 a month or more depending on what development you live in.)
- Where do I dispose of my garbage?
- Has there ever been a mold problem?
- If the house is within a development, who is responsible for maintaining the road? A road in the dry season looks entirely different than in the rainy season. This is important because you might need four-wheel drive to live there.
- Who are the neighbors? Do they own roosters or run a chicken farm?
- What is the elevation? In the rainy season, it may be humid, and this can damage some of your possessions. I've seen guitar necks warp and electronics fail due to the weather. Some of these things are unavoidable but worth considering if you're shipping down expensive items. On some ridges, just a few hundred meters in elevation can make a huge difference.

The Central Valley

What Should I Expect to Pay?

The Central Valley is the area smack in the middle of the country surrounded by several mountain ranges. It includes popular cities such as San José (the capital), Grecia, Sarchi, Atenas, Naranjo, Palmares, and San Ramón. Living in the Central Valley is about thirty percent less expensive than living near a touristy beach area, but that doesn't mean you can't find something affordable at the coast. It's all about doing some legwork, investigating different possibilities, and talking with as many people as you can find.

A rental home in Grecia can start as low as $450 per month and reach upwards into the thousands. Obviously, the larger the home, the more expensive the rent. Rob and I moved to Grecia for its distinguished number of car lots. We were going to buy a car, file some paperwork, stay a few months, and move on with our adventure, but we fell in love with the area. The people were so darn friendly, I believed I was trapped in a *Twilight Zone* episode. That's when you know you've become twisted from the rat race: you're mystified by smiling people.

Living in the Central Valley means you're close to Immigration in San José, the United States and Canadian embassies, motor vehicles, and shopping. And if you're searching for a mall where you can simultaneously shop for a gun and mistakenly spray mace in your face as my husband did, you can find that in the Central Valley. You can read more about that in my first book!

Something that's spectacular about many of these mountainous towns is that they have great weather. And what I mean by great weather is that the temperatures are often in the seventies and low eighties. The downside is there is quite a lengthy rainy season.

Rob and I found cheaper rent by looking for houses that were down long, bumpy dirt roads. One home we rented had us driving through a river! It was a great way to save some money while experiencing a little adventure every time we went to the grocery store. See video link at end of chapter.

The Beach

What Should I Expect to Pay?

Living at the beach, especially in a tourist area, is more expensive than the Central Valley. Monthly rent for a condominium can easily start at $1100, and groceries are pricier too. It seems the farther you travel from San José, the more things cost and the harder they are to find. Whether it's an alternator for your car or a new timer for your dryer, the mechanic will say, "The parts are in San José." But this will be said in Spanish. And you will respond, using your newly learned *español*, "Cuando?" The mechanic will look toward the heavens, shrug, and then retire to the beach for the remainder of the day.

This may deter you right off the bat. You may want to have access to a Denny's or Applebee's. Or buy rear brakes for a Fiat convertible. Don't quote me on the latter. I have no clue if you'll find them in San José. But I can all but guarantee that you will not uncover them next to the pipa fria stand in Brasilito.

The coast also has varying degrees of infrastructure and healthcare. I live in the Northwest Pacific area, known as Guanacaste. We have decent private medical facilities, but our public ones are nothing like the hospitals in the Central Valley. The Caribbean side of the country is still vastly underdeveloped, but boy is it pretty, and the snorkeling is amazing!

There are trade-offs in every area, and some may be game changers for you and your family. But if you find a happy place that feels like home, that may be more important than anything else I've listed.

Links:

Facebook : www.facebook.com/happierthanabillionaire

Airbnb: www.airbnb.com

YouTube Video "Over the River":

https://youtu.be/2xg5TG5luR4

Cell Phones & Wi-Fi

"When you come to a fork in the road... take it."
~ Yogi Berra

I'm happy to report that Costa Rica has come a long way with their internet and cellular coverage. As long as you're not deep in the rainforest, you're likely to find a signal. Costan Rica cell phones work on the GSM network.

Calling Costa Rica from Abroad | Dial International access code 011 (from Canada or US) + 506 (area code) + eight-digit number.
Calling abroad from Costa Rica | Dial 00 + International code 1 (for Canada or US) + area code + phone number

Three Cell Phone Options

1. Use Your Home Provider: If you're only vacationing and don't need a permanent solution, you can usually use your personal cell phone as long as you have a roaming agreement with your provider. Most cellular companies have international roaming plans. For example, Verizon has a "Travel Pass" that charges $10 dollars a day and only charges you for the days you use the service. This will also provide you with a data plan so you can have access to your navigational apps.

2. Bring your UNLOCKED phone & Purchase a SIM Card: There are four phone companies in Costa Rica: ICE/Kolbi, Movistar, TuYo, and Claro. (ICE is also the Costa Rican State Electricity Agency, but it's here where you can purchase a Kolbi SIM card and have it activated.)

You can also purchase SIM cards from kiosks right at the airports. These SIM cards cost $4 and come with prepaid minutes. They can also be bought at grocery stores and other places around the country. Just pop them in your unlocked phone and you're ready to go. But, wait! This is yet another situation where results may vary. I had a guest who bought Kolbi and Claro SIM cards. One only worked on his wife's phone, while the other worked on his. I don't have an explanation for this.

Once you're out of minutes, you can easily add more at many supermarkets, banks, or ICE offices. The rate per minute for local calls is 35 colones. Just hand the number to the cashier at the grocery store, and say the word *recarga* (prepaid). Tell him the amount of colones you want to spend, and which company you bought the SIM card from.

3. Buy a Phone in Costa Rica: You can always stop by an electronics store and buy a phone. Many also sell SIM cards. Phones cost approximately $45 and up.

Don't throw away the SIM card packaging. Your PIN number is on it, and you'll need it to activate your plan!

Internet Calls

With all the advantages of technology, staying in contact with your family is easy and cheap!

Skype: A phone and video-calling internet app. When someone calls you, it will ring your computer or cell phone. My US subscription costs $2.99 per month for unlimited calling to the US and Canada, and $39 per year to maintain a US phone number. For texting, you'll need to purchase Skype credit.

You can always use the free version of Skype. Just have your family download the app onto their cell phone or computer and sign up with a screen name.

Magic Jack: Another internet phone service (no video) and costs $35 per year. It comes with a USB adapter for your computer, but you can download an app for your cell phone. Texts are included in the price.

WhatsApp Messenger: Many people use this app to call or text. In fact, most of my texts and phone calls from Ticos come through this app, so it's worth downloading.

Wi-Fi

Throughout the country, many companies offer Wi-Fi services. We use CRWIFI. My speeds are sufficient for emailing, surfing the web, and both downloading and uploading videos. They have plans starting at $44 per month for 1 Mbps up and 512 Kbps down.

I pay $60 per month for the standard plan , which is 2 Mbps down and 1 Mbps up. In my area the most expensive plan costs $283 per month for 6 Mbps down and 2 Mbps up. (These prices are when billed annually. Your bill will be higher if you decide to pay monthly.)

Depending on where you live, you may be able to access a fiber-optic connection. Every year, there are more options and more companies providing internet service. When deciding on a place to live, make sure to check out what your options will be regarding Wi-Fi service. The days of not being connected to the world are quickly coming to an end in most areas.

Links:

CRWIFI: http://www.crwifi.com
ICE: www.grupoice.com/wps/portal/ICE/Inicio/

Download These Apps!
Skype, Magic Jack,
WhatsApp

Amazon.com: Are We Breaking Up?

"I bet deep down you still wish your mom would take you clothes shopping every August for the new school year."

~ Bridget Willard

Dearest Amazon, how you seduce me with your Prime shipping and sassy deals of the day. You even flashed that toy drone I just Googled five minutes ago. How do you know me so well? It's as if we're soul mates.

But we have a problem. A big one. Costa Rica doesn't have proper addresses, or a good track record when shipping anything to your house It's a crap shoot whether I'll receive it. "Results may vary" is an understatement.

"But I enjoy spinning my own yarn. I'll need to order alpaca wool from Amazon," Hazel states.

You may need to reassess your sweater hobby, Hazel. Plus, it's pretty hot at the beach. But I'm sounding too pessimistic here, so let me stop and share a happy story with you first. I have one friend who ordered from Amazon, and the package shipped to her house in two weeks. What kind of sorcery is this? I do not know. But it all worked out, and she can't speak highly enough about the process. Does that happen to everyone? Oh no, Hazel. That alpaca wool could be held up at customs for a while, and it might never get spun.

PO Boxes & Shipping Services

You may have better luck getting your package delivered if you set up a PO box with Correos de Costa Rica (the Costa Rican Postal Service). Most shipping companies will deliver to one, but sometimes they won't. They'll want your wacky home address, which will be two hundred meters past the mango tree. Remarkably, they may actually find you.

If you're not ordering through Amazon directly from Costa Rica, you can hire an international forwarding service, such as Jetbox or Aeropost. Send your package to their Miami offices. It will set sail on the Love Boat to Costa Rica, drinking margaritas on the promenade deck before getting dumped at a seaport. From there it should be delivered to your door. But that didn't happen for us. We signed up for a shipping service, and they dropped our package off over an hour away like it was some sort of a stowaway.

When you order through Amazon, import taxes are always included on your invoice. Although they will sell anything on their site, some items are restricted for shipment to Costa Rica. You may find you can't order your favorite vitamins or even your special shampoo. It's odd what appears on their no-no list.

Customs Jail

Then you have customs jail, a place where your package is stored for being bad. No one quite knows why some packages are bad and others are not. Once it's flagged, it's up to you to bail it out.

I have a friend who had hundreds of dollars' worth of books stuck at customs. Another friend of mine ordered jeans, and customs jail flagged the package. She had to decide whether it was worth driving three hours, only to spend another couple of hours wrestling with bureaucracy, paying the import tax and storage fee, to retrieve a $50 pair of pants. She decided it wasn't worth it. I still wonder to this day who's wearing them. I bet they look great.

When attempting to claim your package from customs jail, the person it's addressed to must be the one to claim it. Don't send your husband unless he has a notarized letter stating you allow him to up your package. Because, you know, we all walk around with notarized letters from our spouses.

I'm sure in a few years, things will improve. Once Costa Rica gets better with their mail and implements a system of proper addresses, I'm sure we'll all laugh about these stories and reminisce about the good ole days when we traveled three hours and paid $90 for a spiced pumpkin Yankee Candle. But that day is not today.

There are different customs offices around the country, and hopefully, your package will land at the one closest to where you live. For Rob and me, that could be in Puntarenas, a two-hour drive. But it could also arrive at the Panama border or even in San José.

So how do I feel about it all? I'd rather not deal with the stress. This is where the concept of drag comes into play. **Drag is a force acting opposite to the relative motion of any object moving forward.** I felt it all around me when I worked in my office. Things are different now. I live a pretty chill life, and that chillness comes from consciously eliminating things that melt my chill. It means my computer keyboard remains broken until I can wait for a friend to haul one down from the States or I can find someone who repairs it locally. I weaken the drag by reducing its force.

I'm used to living like this, but it could throw others for a loop. Pura Vida is not a "now" lifestyle. It's more like an "Eh, maybe tomorrow" lifestyle or a "Wow, that didn't work out as I planned" lifestyle.

To live here happily, I suggest you decide what's more important to you. Is it quick access to alpaca wool? Or is it the thrill of embarking on a grand adventure? I picked the latter. But then again, my hobby is writing, and I don't need anything more than a pen and a piece of paper. If my hobbies included more than that, I would probably try a little harder to get packages sent to my house.

So, Amazon, I'm not breaking up with you yet, but you really need to work on yourself. I've come to the realization that you can't fulfill my every need, so I'll keep asking people to haul stuff down until you start taking our relationship seriously.

You may not be my soul mate, but you had me at Prime shipping. And I still can't quit you.

Links:

Amazon: www.amazon.com

Correos de Costa Rica: www.correos.go.cr

Jetbox: www.jetbox.com

Aeropost: www.aeropost.com

Tamarindo

Attorneys and Corporations

Gilferd Banton Beckford has been our trusted attorney for over ten years. He's honest, reliable, and an all-around nice guy. This is someone you want to talk to when moving to Costa Rica. And apparently, people are talking to him.

Since being included in my previous *Escape Manual* editions, Gilferd has fielded all sorts of questions from retiring expats looking for a simpler life. One older gentleman called stating he had an appointment that afternoon (he didn't) and wanted to drill Gilferd on many topics. My attorney carved out time, answered his questions, and then realized the man hadn't yet found a place to stay. Gilferd drove the man to a bed and breakfast, made sure he was taken care of, and wished him well.

Has your attorney ever driven you to a bed and breakfast? I bet he hasn't. I wager he puts you on hold, where you're forced to listen to an endless loop of "The Girl from Ipanema." Gilferd will not do that. He simply doesn't have the sophisticated phone system to do so.

Not only Gilferd will carve out time for you, but he genuinely cares if you have a comfortable place to spend the night. I like nice people. And a nice attorney is exactly what you need when buying a car, purchasing a property, or trying to get out of a $500 dollar ticket because you passed a car on a double yellow line.

Vehicle infractions are expensive in Costa Rica. Talking on the phone while driving will cost you $500 dollars. They'll fine you $160 for driving with no seatbelt. Driving without a windshield? Now that's a bargain. It only costs $35 dollars. And guess who actually did that. My husband. In Brooklyn, circa 1988. While most worried about a valid sticker on their windshield, my husband couldn't afford a windshield.

Gilferd can assist you with all of the above, but let me elaborate on the things he will not do for you: launder money, alter your passport, or hide you from your ex-wife. He'll never be rude and will always shake your hand before wishing you a good day. So if you're a normal person, give him a call, but if you're running an illegal high-stakes poker tournament, you may want to look for another attorney.

Another thing he will no longer do is residency applications. He only had two immigration clients. They were my husband and I. The amount of aggravation that followed was too much even for him. No car rides to bed and breakfasts were made.

I recently spoke with Gilferd about opening another corporation. Corporations are a big thing in Costa Rica. Almost everything is purchased through them: cars, houses, weapons, etc. To start one, it can cost anywhere from $300 to $1000.

There are two statuses that can be assigned to corporations: active or inactive. If a corporation is created with the sole purpose of purchasing a high-ticket item, it is usually considered inactive. However, if that asset will be used to create a business, it becomes active.

Here is the rub. You now must pay a yearly tax on each corporation you own, inactive or active. The yearly tax for owning an inactive corporation is $115 and is due every January. So if you have a separate inactive corporation for each of your cars, properties, etc., you end up paying quite a bit of money. They suspended this payment for a couple of years while it was litigated in court. But ultimately the government won, and now every corporation is subjected to this tax.

Active corporation taxes are different. They're based on gross income and vary between $192 and $383. These are also due every January.

The reason everyone places assets in corporations is to provide legal protection. Let's say you're driving without a windshield and someone's prize-winning rooster jumps into your car and gets injured. Since your vehicle is owned by an inactive corporation, the owner couldn't go after your bank account to pay for the rooster's broken wing rehabilitation bills.

But Gilferd says that's no longer the case. Years ago, Costa Rica had no way of knowing who owned these corporations. Today, they do. They know everything. This rooster owner could go after your bank account, or any assets you own. Having a corporation does not provide you the legal coverage it once did.

Where does this leave you? Now that you have to pay $115 on each inactive corporation every year, you may want to think twice about opening one. It's a decision you'll need to talk over with your attorney. There are still many people who believe your assets are much safer in a corporation.

If you do stop by Gilferd's office, please tell him I said hello. Bring my book and ask him to sign it. You'll be happy you did. We were lucky to have met him all those years ago, and he continues to enlighten us regarding complex issues.

Also, ask him about his time growing up on the Caribbean coast of Costa Rica. A place where he played in turquoise water, watched toucans fly overhead, and had barefoot picnics under palm trees. While this is a dream for most, it was just an ordinary childhood for him.

I believe that's why he's so kind to us gringos who have landed in a confusing land. He can still hear the calming rustle of palm trees and feel the Caribbean breeze at his back. And it may be the reason he cares where you lay your head when you visit his beautiful country.

Lic. Gilferd Banton Beckford

Attorney at Law

250 metros sur de la Municipalidad de Grecia, Costa Rica

Cell: 8896-7910

Buying or Shipping a Car

"To attract men, I wear a perfume called 'New Car Interior.'"

~ Rita Rudner

Should you buy or import a car? There are pros and cons to each. Either way, it's likely to cost the same amount of money.

Buying a Car in Costa Rica

When deciding on a car, you'll want one that is prevalent in Costa Rica so that you can easily find parts. We bought our Mitsubishi Montero because we saw so many on the road. I have a friend who purchased a Korean car and couldn't even find a side-view mirror replacement. As a result, he couldn't pass inspection.

I always recommend purchasing an SUV, especially if you plan on exploring the country. A compact car is okay, but there will be situations in which four-wheel drive is necessary. That said, Ticos with compact cars do not have problems getting where they need to go. Whether it be through a river or up a cliff, they just say a prayer and keep going. We've stopped at river banks, wondering if it was safe to cross, only to have a Tico in a Yugo drive right past us and straight into the water. They chug through like Chitty Chitty Bang Bang.

A lawyer is necessary to confirm the title is clean and to prepare documents for the National Registry. The buyer is responsible for the transfer tax of 2.5% and registration fee of .05% of the purchase price. Both parties split the lawyer fees.

Shipping Your Car

Shipping a car can be ideal since you already know the condition of the vehicle. There'll be no surprises unless it gets damaged during shipping. Many people think they can import a junker to save money, but Costa Rica doesn't want it here and they will apply a higher tax. So sell that Chevy Nova and use the funds to purchase a newer vehicle.

You will have to pay import taxes on the car once it arrives, and they will be a lot. In the end, that vehicle will likely cost the same as if you bought it in Costa Rica.

Car Import Tax	Motorcycle Import Tax
0–3 years old....52.29%,	0–3 years old....58.10%
4–5 years old....63.91%	4–5 years old....46.48%
6 + years old.....79.03%	6+ years old.....34.85%

Taxes

Let's do some math. Let's say you bought a five-year-old used car for $10,000 and are shipping it to Costa Rica. The shipping alone will cost about $1,500.

Customs officials will use the Valuation Database of the Ministry of the Treasury (Cartica/Autovalor) to determine their value of the car. If it's more than what you claim to have paid, they will use the higher number. Now let's say Costa Rican officials have valued your car at $12,000. The car mentioned above is five years old, so we must calculate taxes according to that age.

$12,000 (value) x 63.91% (tax for a five-year-old car) = a whopping import tax of $7,669.20

After $7,669.20 in import taxes plus the $1500 it cost to ship it, this suddenly no longer sounds like a such a great deal. You also need to consider the shape your car will be in when it finally arrives. I have friends that had their cars damaged during shipping and said they would never do it again. I have other friends that received their cars in pristine condition.

If you are in love with your car, and it fits your needs in Costa Rica, by all means, consider shipping it. Barry the Shipper can even get it inspected and registered and have it waiting at the airport for you! He will need the following documents before shipping:

Vehicle Shipping Checklist

- ☐ Vehicle title from your home country
- ☐ Proof of Vehicle Identification Number
- ☐ Original invoice showing purchase of car
- ☐ Current emissions test certificate

Once the vehicle is in Costa Rica, you will be granted a temporary title that is good for 48 hours. You must immediately take your car to be inspected at Riteve and pay for your registration at any INS office.

Registration (Marchamo)

In order for your car to be legal, you need to have a proper registration (*marchamo*). This piece of paper is kept in your glove compartment, with a coordinating sticker you place on your windshield. It's mandatory and needs to be renewed every December. You can pay this at any INS office, Banco de Costa Rica, or Banco Nacional. After January 1, not having a valid registration is a common reason for traffic police to pull you over, and it's a huge deal in Costa Rica. Fines are expensive, and you may even have your car towed away.

A valid marchamo not only serves as one's registration but also includes mandatory-minimal insurance that would compensate anyone who is killed or injured in the event that you're involved in an accident. Additional insurance is available through INS (National Insurance Institute). These private plans cover collision, theft, fire, etc.

How much will you pay for a marchamo? Call toll free 800-Marchamo, or send a text message to 1467 with the word *marchamo,* followed by the plate number. Or you can find this information on the INS website.

Inspection (Riteve)

Unlike a marchamo, which is due every December, a car's inspection date is determined by the last digit on your license plate. After you pass inspection, they award you a sticker (and trust me, it feels like an award after going through the process) that gets adhered to your windshield.

A car must be inspected prior to paying the marchamo. All outstanding tickets must be paid.

Car inspection is performed at Riteve, and it costs around $30. There are many of these facilities scattered throughout the country. Schedule an appointment via the Riteve website.

The inspection process in Costa Rica is a very stressful endeavor. A car can fail for just about anything, including a slight oil leak. Our car failed for an abrasive noise coming from the engine. The car is twenty years old. What were they expecting?

A contemporary jazz solo? Everything about the car is abrasive. I get abrasive just climbing into the passenger seat.

It's amazing how little Rob and I knew when we first moved to Costa Rica. We were a nutty couple with a dream and a stack of money in my husband's underwear. We knew little about what we needed to purchase, inspect, or insure a car. But it all worked out, and that car took us to every corner of the country.

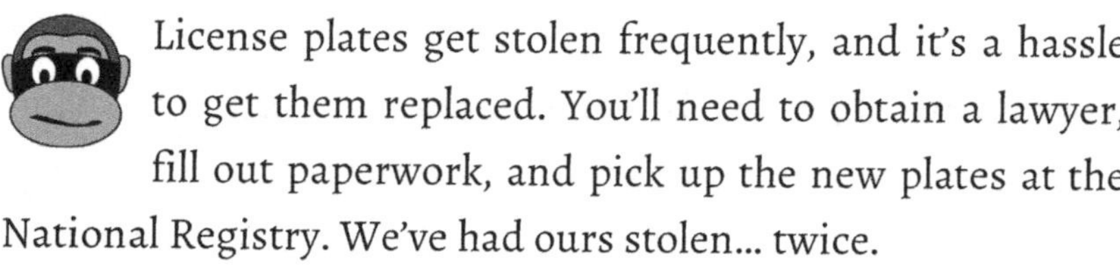

License plates get stolen frequently, and it's a hassle to get them replaced. You'll need to obtain a lawyer, fill out paperwork, and pick up the new plates at the National Registry. We've had ours stolen... twice.

Links:

Calculate the value of your car: https://serviciosnet.hacienda.go.cr/autohacienda/

INS: http://www.ins-cr.com

Riteve (inspection station for your car): www.rtv.co.cr/

Getting A Driver's License

REPUBLICA DE COSTA RICA
Licencia de Conducir
Nº: DM-146333321111
Expedición 31-9-2018
Nacimiento 11-06-2014
Vencimiento 19-10-2021
Tipo: B1
Bugsy
R.F.
R.T.
T.S.
Willoughby III Bugsy

"Never lend your car to anyone to whom you have given birth."

~ Erma Bombeck

You've shipped your car, paid the tax, and gotten it registered, and you're ready to hit the road. The only thing left is your Costa Rican driver's license. Here is the rub:

You can't get a Costa Rican driver's license without a *cédula* (your legal residency ID card). Even your *tramite* (document stating that your residency process has begun and is under review) will not be accepted. Where does this leave you? An expat without a Costa Rican driver's license can still drive using two documents: a valid driver's license from their home country, and their visa that has been stamped within the last 90 days. After 90 days, expats must leave the country to renew their visas. It is not legal to drive with an expired visa.

Obtaining a Driver's License Checklist

- ☐ Several copies of your home country driver's license, front and back, translated into Spanish by an approved translator.
- ☐ Two copies of your cédula front and back.
- ☐ Two copies of your passport front page, and the visa stamp reflecting that you have been in the country for at least 91 consecutive days.
- ☐ Proof of payment for driver's license ($12). It's best to pay this first at the Bank of Costa Rica, and be sure to take the receipt when you go to COSEVI. The La Uruca office now has a payment facility right after you walk past the gate. If you're a senior citizen, you can go to the front of the line like a rock star.
- ☐ When getting their first Costa Rican driver's licenses, many people are told they must go to the La Uruca COSEVI facility near San José on Highway 108. Official information states that COSEVI is now allowing people to apply at local branches. But results may vary. My friend Michelle was able to get hers at the local COSEVI facility in Liberia. I have another friend who was declined in Liberia and told they must apply at the La Uruca office. I would suggest that, after obtaining residency, you go directly to the closest COSEVI branch and give it a shot there first.
- ☐ You'll need a medical exam. That's right, folks, a medical exam. You can get this at your local doctor, or even one of the many facilities located right outside the COSEVI.

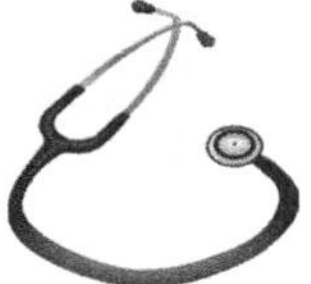

I remember pulling into a parking lot near the La Uruca facility where a man was holding up a dirty piece of cardboard. I thought it read "stranger danger," but Rob insisted it was directing us toward a medical office.

"How bad can it be?" Rob said after parking the car. We then walked through the garage bay to find a waiting room in a dark corner. Next to a row of plastic chairs stood a decapitated mannequin wearing dirty corduroy shorts.

"Stop worrying," Rob urged. "We found the right place."

He was right; I was overreacting. I tend to do that when imagining someone wearing my skin as a cape. Happily, the office visit did not involve dumping my body into a twenty-foot hole. Hannibal Lecter was actually a nice doctor who swiftly made sure I met the rudimentary requirements to drive a car.

The exam only lasted ten minutes. The physician smiled, explained that I'd passed, then shook my hand like a banker would after approving a commercial loan. I felt important. Apparently, finding out you are not blind and can sit at a 90-degree angle is quite the accomplishment.

This medical exam costs between $30 and $40. You don't receive any paperwork, only an email confirmation that's linked with COSEVI's database.

Congratulations! Your medical exam no longer requires a blood test. When Rob gave his blood sample at a doctor's office, he almost passed out. All the young Ticas came to his aid, handed him fluids, and all but rocked him to sleep. When I got pricked, I didn't even get a Band-Aid.

Once you get to COSEVI and present all of the necessary paperwork, you'll eventually receive your driver's license. Why do I say eventually? Because the machine that prints out your card will jam. Repeatedly. Many employees will stand around it, shaking their heads, before realizing it's lunchtime. When the woman returns, she'll have a very flirtatious conversation with Diego the card machine fixer. Diego will return her overtures by ceasing to repair anything. Just keep your cool. You'll eventually get your card, which will be good for **three years**. You'll then celebrate by cramming twelve friends into the car and blasting Madonna on the radio. Which is precisely what I did when I got my license as a teenager.

You should arrive at COSEVI early in the morning. The hours to obtain a driver's license may vary between branches. The La Uruca facility hours are between 8 a.m. and 12 p.m. on Tuesdays and Wednesdays.

Renewing Your License

This can be done at various MOPT (Ministries of Public Works and Transportation) agencies around the country: Liberia, Limón, San Ramón, etc. You'll need a new medical exam, your cédula, and another proof of payment receipt ($12). Everything goes so much faster. A renewed license is good for **six years.**

Once Rob lost his license, and when he tried to get another one, the clerk informed him that his card was fraudulent. How did this happen? When we renewed our licenses a year before in San Ramon, the electricity had gone out just as the clerk was typing our information into the system. So instead he wrote our new license numbers in a Dora the Explorer composition book. "Pura vida," he said, after promising that he would enter the information into the system once the lights came back on. He didn't. And thinking back, I remember that he was doodling in the same notebook. That's never a good sign.

The most important thing to take from this chapter is that it will all work out. Once you get your residency, you'll be able to get a legal Costa Rican license. You'll drive these pothole-ridden roads with impunity and never look back.

Links:

Official Translators: www.rree.go.cr/?sec=servicios&cat=informacion&cont=1054

COSEVI: www.csv.go.cr

MOPT: www.mopt.go.cr

Dominicalito

Education

"It's easier to floss with barbed wire than admit you like someone in middle school."

~ Laurie Halse Anderson

There are many reasons families move abroad, but the main one is to experience living in a new culture. We get stuck in our comfort zone, so becoming an expat is a welcomed jolt of energy. It isn't long before you're viewing the world—and your part in it—differently. I'm still amazed at the things I'm learning each and every day.

It's shocking not only how quickly children adapt to a new culture but also how easily they can learn a new language. I've seen some become fluent in only a few months; it's the adults that have a harder time. In most cases, children end up tutoring their parents! I think I may need to have some kids.

Because of reliable internet connections, people are now able to work remotely, and many choose to do it with their feet in the sand. If you had the option to work anywhere in the world, would it be where you are now?

Finding the right school is important, and it may determine where you end up. Should you move to the beach or the mountains? Should you live in a metropolitan area, or are you longing for open spaces?

At the coast, you'll have a variety of choices. The schools in my area are filling up. What started out as a family's twelve-month sojourn has turned into a place they now call home. Moving to Costa Rica isn't such a crazy idea anymore. It's a real option for many families.

Types of Diplomas

There are three different types of diplomas a child can obtain in Costa Rica, depending on what school they're attending:

The National Baccalaureate/Diploma of Costa Rica, accredited by the Ministry of Education (MEP).

Public and private: Students must pass tests proving they have met all MEP requirements. If you decide to move back to your home country, parents can easily enroll their child back into school since the child was receiving a government-accredited education. This diploma is also accepted by many colleges.

The International Baccalaureate Diploma (IB), accredited by the IBO in Geneva, Switzerland

An IB diploma is a two-year educational program (11th and 12th grade) providing qualification for admission to college. It is highly regarded around the world.

The United States High School Diploma, accredited by the Southern Association of Colleges and Schools (SACS)

An SACS is a United States accreditation, and students will receive a typical high school diploma.

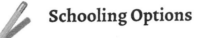

Schooling Options

- **Costa Rica Public School** | No Cost | MEP Certification

You can enroll your child in the Costa Rican public school system, but all lessons are taught in Spanish. Teachers are rarely available to assist non-Spanish-speaking children. If your child is already bilingual, this is a promising option.

- **Catholic School** | $200+ per month | MEP Certification

Private Catholic schools are located throughout Costa Rica and are MEP-certified. However, they're Spanish-speaking schools, and it could be a challenge for an English-speaking student.

- **Alternative School** | $300+ per month | For children who have learning challenges or who are uncomfortably smart, there are alternative schools. They are not MEP-certified but will prepare students for MEP testing. These schools get children where they need to go; they just take a different route getting there.

• **Homeschooling** | $500+ per year | Your home country's certification (such as an SACS if you're from the United States) Homeschooling is becoming more popular with families, especially ones moving abroad. Regulations and guidelines differ depending on what state or province you had lived in back home. You'll need to check with your home town's education department. Meeting these requirements will allow your child to have the same accreditation as if she had gone through the public school.

There are now many online homeschooling programs, and with some research, you'll find one which suits your child best. There are additional costs involved, resources to buy, and evaluation fees, but it's an affordable way to enroll your child in an accredited curriculum.

It won't take long to find other homeschooled families in Costa Rica, and they have an incredible support system. There are plenty of activities in which they have the opportunity to mingle with children from other schools in the area. Many private schools have extracurricular activities open to all children in the community.

• **Private School** | $600+ per month | Depending on their curriculum, private schools may provide your child with an IB, SACS, or similar diploma. One advantage to this is that there is a strong possibility of obtaining a high school diploma equivalent to those awarded in the country you're originally from. There are even French schools in the Central Valley.

Two popular private schools in my area are La Paz Community School and CRIA. The former is located at the entrance of my community. I love watching the children ride their bicycles to school every morning. There is one girl, in particular, I see on my daily walks, who always yells, "Buenos dias!" as she flies past me on her ten-speed. I admire how she manages the hills, flying in the face of it all, just enjoying being a kid.

One thing I hope you take away from this chapter is that you are not crazy to want to give your children a different view of the world. And you wouldn't be the first. There are wonderful communities here, and the families work together to make children feel loved and accepted.

Links:

Central Valley Schools:

- Country Day School: www.cds.ed.cr
- Pan-American School: www.panam.ed.cr
- Int. Christian School: www.facebook.com/icscostarica

Guanacaste Schools:

- La Paz Community School: www.lapazschool.org
- CRIA: www.criacademy.com

Costa Rica Ministry of Education: www.mep.go.cr

Motmot

Banks and ATMs

"People are living longer than ever before, a phenomenon undoubtedly made necessary by the 30-year mortgage."
~ Doug Larson

Banks in Costa Rica have improved drastically. Wait times have decreased significantly, but don't expect to be in and out of there when they're busy. Banco de Costa Rica and Banco Nacional are state-run banks, and you'll see them throughout the country. These are the most popular since they are intertwined with government entities, and you'll be visiting them often. There are also private institutions such as Citibank, BAC Credomatic, Banco Popular, HSBC, and Scotiabank.

Inside the Bank

Many state-run banks now have kiosks right inside their lobby. Tap the icon labeled *CAJA* on the display. The next screen will show icons asking if you are doing one or more than one transaction. Hit the correct icon, and a ticket will slide out from a slot below. If you need to talk to a bank teller about opening an account, hit the button that reads *Platforma*.

If the bank doesn't have a kiosk, they'll probably have a ticket dispenser similar to what you may find in a bakery. Either way, there will be a screen on the wall that displays a number corresponding to the next person in line. When it's your turn, the system will call your number out loud. This is a great place to learn Spanish numbers!

If the bank doesn't have a kiosk or ticket dispenser, then you're in for a little exercise. As a teller becomes available, every person will stand up and shift down a seat. It's the bankers' version of musical chairs.

Exchanging Money

Easy breezy! Just inform the teller, "*Me gustaría cambiar dinero.*" (I would like to exchange money.) The key word is *cambiar*. If you just say that, they'll know what you mean. I can't tell you how many times I've said one verb and Ticos instantly understood why I was standing in front of them looking clueless.

ATMS

Many ATMs now have prompts in English. There may be an ATM charge of up to $5 and possibly a 2.5–3% international withdrawal fee from your bank at home. Give your bank a call and see if they'll waive the fee. It's also important to let them know you're traveling abroad so they don't flag your transactions as fraudulent. Do this with your credit cards as well. ATMs are closed between 10 p.m. and 5 a.m.

Ripped or raggedy money will not be accepted by most vendors. Fifty- and hundred-dollar bills may be difficult to break in some locations, but you can do this at any bank.

You can usually withdraw more money per transaction at a Banco Nacional than at a Banco de Costa Rica. This will save you from being charged multiple transaction fees.

When making deposits for residency purposes, it's important to request an official printout of your monthly deposits. When it's time to renew your temporary residency, you'll need to show these records. Costa Rican banks don't keep them for long, so to be on the safe side, ask for them every three months.

Opening a Bank Account

Congratulations! You can now open a bank account in Costa Rica without being a resident. We've come a long way, baby!

I went to Bank of Costa Rica for the following information, so it's possible that other banks may request additional information. Bank of Costa Rica is a good banking option since some bills can only be paid there, and anytime you have to deposit money into a government account, it will likely be through Bank of Costa Rica.

There are two different types of accounts you can open at Bank of Costa Rica, each with different requirements: personal account or corporate account.

Personal Bank Account Checklist

- ☐ Passport
- ☐ Costa Rican telephone number
- ☐ Costa Rican address
- ☐ Email

Easy breezy, right? However, there is one noteworthy restriction with this type of account. You cannot perform online transactions between other Costa Rican banks. If you're out of the country and need to pay your rent, you cannot transfer money online from your Costa Rican account into theirs.

This is a recent change and came as a shock to many. Without any advance notice, people suddenly could not pay their bills online anymore.

To remedy this, instead of opening a personal bank account, many people hire an attorney and create a corporation. As stated earlier, it's common to have your home, car, weapons, etc., in separate Costan Rica corporations. You may already have one if you own a piece of land or a house here. If you already own several corporations, be careful not to use the one that includes your car. Never attach your car corporation to anything else. It may cause complications in the event of a car accident.

Corporate Bank Account Checklist

- ☐ Passport
- ☐ Costa Rican telephone number
- ☐ Address
- ☐ Email
- ☐ The ID number of the corporation you wish to use
- ☐ Corporation papers listing the owners of the company

"That wasn't a big deal at all," Jim tells Hazel. "People complain a lot about banking in Costa Rica when it's really straightforward."

I'll tell you why people complain, Jim. Have you or Hazel tried moving money from your home country into Costa

Rica? That's where it can get complicated. Whether you have a personal or corporate account, moving money can be one big headache.

When a large sum of money gets transferred into your Costa Rican account, the bank won't release it unless you show the origins of the money. Usually, that includes a current bank statement from your home country that has your name and bank account number on it. If you're in Costa Rica, that obviously will not be mailed to you. You can print an online statement, but for security reasons, those don't have your full account number at the top.

The purpose of all this is to prove that you and Hazel are not Colombian drug lords, terrorists, or good old-fashioned white-collar money launderers. And to be honest, Jim, you've got a shifty look about you. I'd let Hazel talk to the bank teller if I were you.

When we built our home, we waited weeks for money transfers to go through and spent even more time trying to convince them I was just some dopey author that wanted to build a house. They got the dopey part right away, but they still wanted to see my paperwork.

Every.

Single.

Time.

This can quickly get old and frustrating. When you encounter situations like this, take a deep breath and remember why you moved here in the first place. If you're like me, you fell in love with Costa Rica's swirly lavender sunsets. I've witnessed some that resembled vibrant chalk paintings drawn on Paris sidewalks.

These are the best cure for frustrating days at the bank. You won't need to stand in line or take a ticket. You're an expat now and have a front-row seat every night.

Links:

Banco de Costa Rica: www.bancobcr.com
Banco Nacional: www.bncr.fi.cr

Residency

"A pessimist sees only the dark side of the clouds, and mopes; a philosopher sees both sides, and shrugs; an optimist doesn't see the clouds at all — he's walking on them."

~ Leonard Louis Levinson

I'm glad you opened this chapter; it may be the most important in the entire manual. This is when things get real. Every person who has applied for residency has a story to tell. For some, it went smoothly, for others it was a hassle, but either way, choosing to apply for it is an important decision.

Your residency status will affect your ability to drive, how often you need to leave the country, and whether or not you can work. A big change came a few years ago, when Costa Rica prohibited nonresidents from getting a Costa Rican driver's license. Even those with residency applications waiting for approval are denied. These individuals (often referred to as perpetual tourists) are still able to drive using their home country driver's license in conjunction with a valid 90-day visa stamp on their passports.

With that said, it may be in your best interest to get residency, especially if you're buying property and/or staying awhile. When I received mine, I showed every Tico I met. I planted a tiny Costa Rican flag to my dashboard and yelled, "Yo soy una Tica!" I may have even flashed it to the gas station attendant.

I excitedly showed my gastroenterologist. It was imperative the guy doing my colonoscopy appreciate that my colon has dual nationality. No flags were planted.

Residency Categories

Pensionado (Retiree) Requires that applicants have proof of a monthly pension of at least $1,000. Only one pension is necessary for a married couple. Pension plans can include Social Security, 401k, IRA, and lifetime annuities.
No monthly Costa Rican bank deposits are required.

Rentista (Legal Resident) This category is a little more complicated. It requires that an applicant show proof of unearned income. What is unearned income? One of the most common forms is a certificate of deposit.

The current minimal unearned income requirement is $2,500 per month for two years ($60,000). Based on this, the applicant must provide a bank letter stating that he or she has at least $60,000 in a "stable and permanent" manner. This amount will cover the applicant, spouse, and any children under twenty-five years old.

There is a required Costa Rican bank deposit. Once you become a temporary resident, you must move $2500 into a Costa Rican bank every month for two years.

Inversionista (Investment) This category requires a higher level of commitment. The applicant must invest at least $200,000 in a business, the purchase of a home, commercial real estate, or land used for preservation purposes.

The property value of your investment must be registered with the local municipality. The assessed value of the property must be at least $200,000. No monthly Costa Rican bank deposits are required.

Vinculo (Marriage Relation) Marry someone or have your child born in Costa Rica. This is the only category that allows you to legally work before obtaining permanent residency.

Any of the methods listed above can lead you to temporary residency. After three years you can apply for permanent residency, a process which is much easier.

Marcia Solís, The Residency Professional

Applying for residency was a challenging experience for us. It was the first residency case our attorney filed, and the last. The miscommunication between institutions continually surprised him. For example, we deposited a fee into a government account listed on our residency paperwork. When we got to immigration, they said our money was deposited into the wrong account.

"But the account number is listed here," our attorney said, "right on the papers you handed me."

"It's wrong," the clerk said. And wrong in Costa Rica means it took us weeks before we could get our money back and deposit it into the correct account. After a year, we finally got our temporary residency and our attorney said he'll never do it again.

That's why you should hire someone who does this for a living, someone who knows the ins and outs of the immigration vortex. For many, that woman is Marcia Solís from Send Me South (www.sendmesouth.com). Having her on your side should make this process much easier.

Marcia is an attorney and residency specialist. She's helped many gringos get their cédulas without losing their minds. I've lost mine (my mind, not my cédula) in many Costa Rican government offices, while my husband casually bought Coca-Cola from vending machines. He can stay calm no matter how thick the bureaucracy. But not so much after purchasing imitation ricotta or mozzarella cheese. That sets this superhero off.

I contacted Marcia to see if she had any advice for people looking to start the process, and she was kind enough to answer some questions.

Do you think it's important to file? Many people do border runs for years. Why should they bother getting their cédula?

"How long are you planning to stay? That is the question you need to ask yourself. If the person is staying for less than one year, I truly believe it is no use to apply for residency.

"However, if someone is planning on staying three years or more, then it's better to apply. I suggest this because rules keep changing, and now there is a new regulation that states perpetual tourists (people who keep going over the border every 90 days) are subject to being granted less than 90 days between border runs. They will also have to pay a ticket of $100 before they can reenter the country. This does not apply to every perpetual tourist but is randomly applied at airports and borders. So this means it is a matter of bad luck if you get selected."

This is official proof that results may vary, and you're not just paranoid. It happened to my girlfriend. She did her usual crossing over the border but was only able to renew her visa for 15 days. She was a perpetual tourist for years with no problems. It's always at the discretion of the border agents to decide how many days you're allowed in the country.

"Hence, by applying for residency," Marcia continued, "applicants are free to stay in Costa Rica once their application is on file with immigration. There is no need to leave every 90 days to update their tourist visa because they are in a standby position, waiting for the government's approval. Also, after three years as a temporary resident, they can apply for permanent residency."

What type of problems do you run into?

"Sometimes my clients forget documents, or some of their papers don't have an apostille stamp. Some documents have already expired. The good thing is that this does not happen often. If they have any questions, I am here to assist them."

What is the time frame?

"I am very clear with my clients right from the beginning not to expect any news for 10 to 12 months after submitting their applications. Migración does not approve any before that timeframe."

Have you had any issues with Migración?

"The only issue I have had in the past is that Migración took longer than expected to accept an application. In this case, I filed a claim, and within a month and a half, the application was accepted.

"Again, the key to success is to submit everything correctly from the beginning. That is the one thing I want everyone to remember."

Various Residency Fees

There are several payments to be made.

- $255 per applicant: government fees
- $60 per translation: official translations into Spanish for birth certificate, criminal record, marriage certificate, financial solvency letter, etc.
- $150 per applicant: Special Power issued by a local notary to process applications at Migración
- $45 each: authentication of signatures of the Affiliation Form and Application Letter.
- The residency attorney of your choice will charge a fee. Send Me South charges $800 per person (with discounts for families) to take care of everything until Migración approves applications. They will also arrange appointments for picking up residency cards.

The Apostille Stamp

If you are from the United States, each of your documents (birth certificate, marriage license, etc.) will need an apostille stamp. You can obtain this by sending each paper to the Secretary of State from which each document originated. (For example, if you were born in New Jersey, you'll need to send that birth certificate to New Jersey's Secretary of State.)

An apostille is a pretty gold star stamped on documents that proves their authenticity. It applies to all countries who are members of the Hague Convention, and many countries abide by these guidelines. But not Canada, you little vixens. Don't you want gold stars on your documents, eh? Us Americans love our stars. We even put them on our flag. But I am impressed with your old-school commitment to document authentication. It's like keeping high-wasted jeans in style. So for all you Canucks out there, you must take the documents to your Costa Rican consulate and then get them authenticated at the Ministry of Foreign Affairs in San José.

Marcia's Residency Checklist

Regardless of which type of residency you are applying for, each applicant will need the following documents:

- ☐ Birth Certificate: Valid for only 6 months from issued date. This document must be notarized and apostilled in your country of origin. Please take note that if you're from a country that is not a member of the Hague Con-

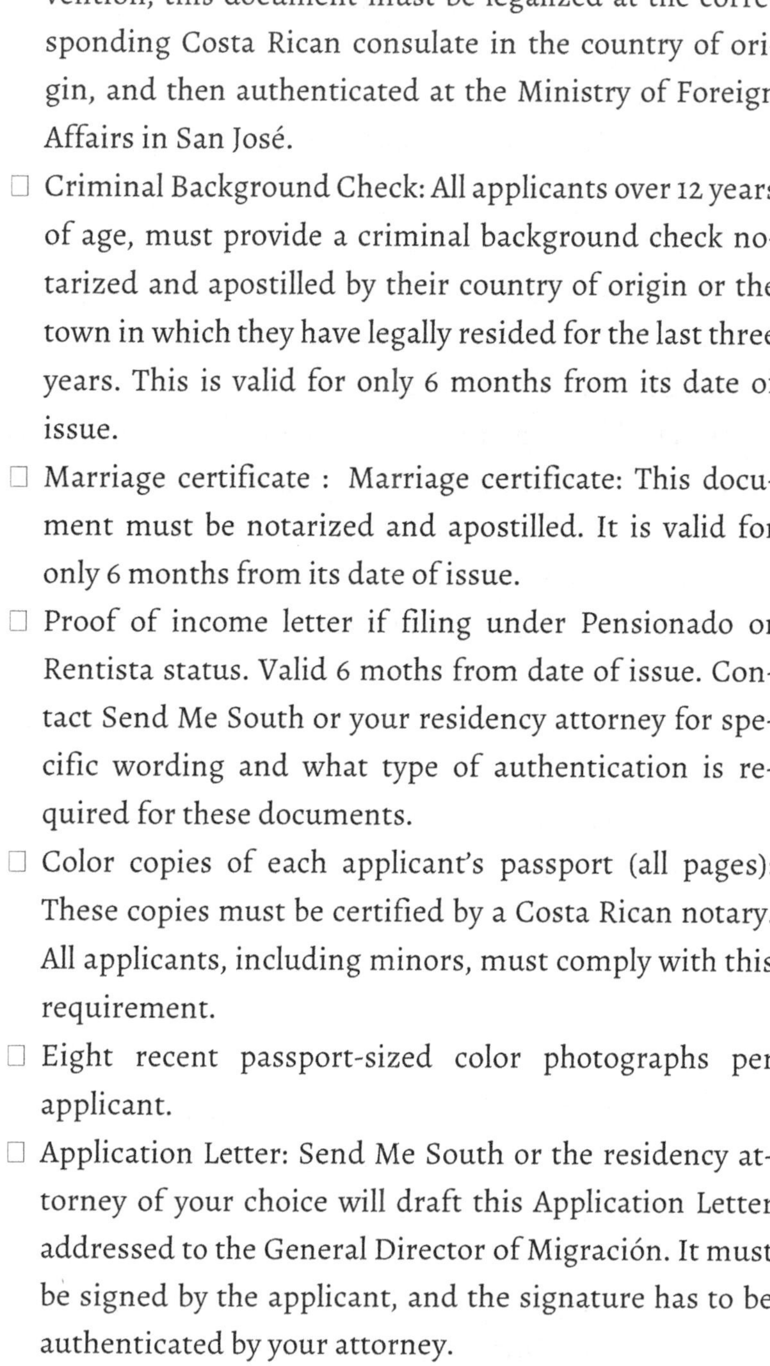

vention, this document must be legalized at the corresponding Costa Rican consulate in the country of origin, and then authenticated at the Ministry of Foreign Affairs in San José.

- ☐ Criminal Background Check: All applicants over 12 years of age, must provide a criminal background check notarized and apostilled by their country of origin or the town in which they have legally resided for the last three years. This is valid for only 6 months from its date of issue.
- ☐ Marriage certificate : Marriage certificate: This document must be notarized and apostilled. It is valid for only 6 months from its date of issue.
- ☐ Proof of income letter if filing under Pensionado or Rentista status. Valid 6 moths from date of issue. Contact Send Me South or your residency attorney for specific wording and what type of authentication is required for these documents.
- ☐ Color copies of each applicant's passport (all pages): These copies must be certified by a Costa Rican notary. All applicants, including minors, must comply with this requirement.
- ☐ Eight recent passport-sized color photographs per applicant.
- ☐ Application Letter: Send Me South or the residency attorney of your choice will draft this Application Letter addressed to the General Director of Migración. It must be signed by the applicant, and the signature has to be authenticated by your attorney.

- ☐ Affiliation Form: This is a form processed by Send Me South or your residency attorney on your behalf. It must be signed by the applicant and authenticated by a local notary.
- ☐ A special Power of Attorney: This must be granted to Send Me South or the residency attorney of your choice before any document can be submitted to Migración on the applicant's behalf.
- ☐ Proof of Consular Registration: This shows the intention of applying for residency in Costa Rica. Please note: This requirement does not apply if the applicant's country of origin does not have a consulate or embassy in Costa Rica. When this is the case, the applicant must send a formal request to the Ministry of Foreign Affairs of Costa Rica.
- ☐ Fingerprint Registration: This must be done by all applicants, including children over twelve, in San José or Liberia.

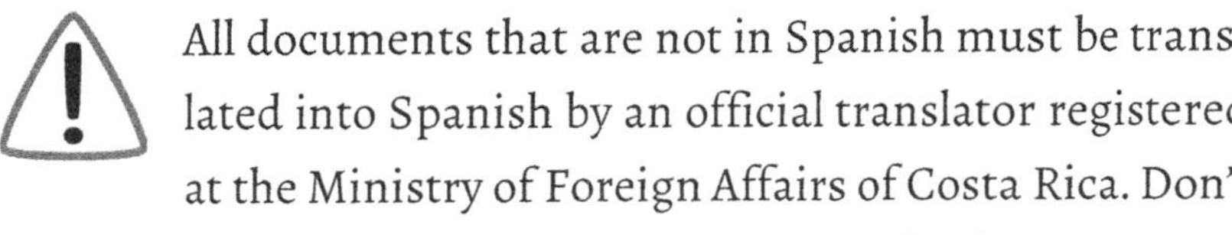

All documents that are not in Spanish must be translated into Spanish by an official translator registered at the Ministry of Foreign Affairs of Costa Rica. Don't make the mistake of hiring someone not on this list.

Considerations

- Each applicant will be assigned a file number at Migración, and parents must sign all documents on behalf of minors.
- If for any reason the applicant cannot obtain any of the needed documents (birth certificate, criminal record,

etc.), the individual must present an affidavit stating such reasons.

- All applicants must be in Costa Rica with a valid tourist visa at the moment their applications are submitted at Migración.
- Once residency is approved, applicants (now residents) must begin to contribute to Caja Costarricense de Seguro Social (C.C.S.S.). Your monthly bill will be based on the income you reported in your application. These payments will not only give you access to the public health care system but also entitle you to Costa Rican social security later.

Links:

Marcia Solís at Send Me South

(506) 2221-1540 office

(506) 8887-1853 cell

www.sendmesouth.com

Dirección de Migración y Extrangeria

www.migracion.go.cr

Border Runs

"Of all the books in the world, the best stories are found between the pages of a passport."

~ Unknown

Costa Rican border runs have a certain quality to them. A sense of adventure mixed with a healthy dose of confusion. Many expats have been doing this for years, and we call these lively characters perpetual tourists.

A typical Costa Rica visa is **valid for 90 days**, and if you don't have residency, you will need to leave before it expires. You must also leave if you have filed for residency but have not yet received your tramite (the official paper stating that your residency application is being processed).

How long should you spend time over the border before returning? Just an hour or so. Is that an absolute fact worthy of entry into the *Escape Manual*? Unequivocally not. If you were planning on writing any mean emails to me, now would be a great time to start. I'll even write one for you so you can copy and paste.

What a piece of work. She said I only needed to spend one hour over the border, but they made me stay two. Thanks for nothing, Nadine. P.S. You're not funny.

Chuck, from Jerktown, USA

Some expats walk across, turn around and come straight back. Others were told to stay two hours. We used to stay for a few days because it was fun, and we made a mini vacation out of it. All or none of these may be right. Border rules are peculiar and never absolute. Currently people are walking across, staying for an hour, and returning.

If you plan on driving your car across the border, you will need to obtain a $15 vehicle exit permit (*Permiso de Salida*) from Costa Rica's National Registry. You will also need to show your vehicle's title at the border. **You cannot drive a rental car across the border.**

If you drive up to the border, be aware that there may be a very long line of trucks. You can go around them, which will mean you're driving into oncoming traffic. It's a real-life Frogger video game, but with higher stakes. Once at the border, you go to a designated window to get your car's paperwork stamped. Once over the border, you need to buy car insurance that will cover you while driving in that country.

Panama Border Crossings

Sixaola-Guabito: 7:00 a.m. to 6:00 p.m.
By far, this is one of the weirdest border crossings. It's on the Caribbean side of the country, and a perfect place to cross if you're near the popular tourist town of Puerto Viejo and want to visit Panama's archipelago of Bocas del Toro.

They used to have a rickety old railway bridge with only wooden planks running across rusted steel beams. I once asked someone if it was safe to drive across, "Sure," he said, "it's been here over a hundred years." Not the vote of confidence one looks for when planning on living long enough to cross it.

It looked like a scene out of an *Indiana Jones* movie: boards crackling and debris falling into the river below as we drove across. Luckily for you, the bridge has been replaced with an asphalt road. Now when walking across, you squeeze to the side as an eighteen-wheeler whizzes by inches from your delicate bodily organs. It seems they solved one problem by replacing it with another.

Paso Canoas: 7:00 am to 11:00 p.m. Mon – Fri | 7:00 a.m. to 9:00 p.m. Sat & Sun.

This border is on the Pan-American highway and is the busiest of the three. It's where you'll want to cross if you're headed to David, Boquete, or Panama City. There are long wait times and many people running up to you to offer help getting across. If you don't speak Spanish, these individuals can speed things up. But be aware, they are not official, and never, ever hand them your passport. If it gets stolen, you have a long day ahead of you. Use their services at your own risk.

Rio Sereno: 7:00 a.m. to 11:00 p.m.
This border is located in the mountains and probably the least crowded. Make sure you have all your paperwork lined up before heading there since there are few resources n the area.

Remember that Panama is one hour ahead. Always check border hours (and their lunch break) before starting this trip.

Panama Border Fees

Leaving Costa Rica

- $7 Costa Rica Exit Fee (keep that receipt handy)
- $3 Panama Entry Fee

Car Fees

- $15 insurance if driving your car across
- $1 Fumigation Fee: Only for your car. If they fumigate you, send me a selfie #nofilter.

Returning To Costa Rica

- $3 Panama Exit Fee
- No Costa Rica Entry Fee

Nicaragua Border Crossings

Penas Blancas: 6:00 a.m. to 10:00 p.m. Mon – Fri | 6:00 a.m. to 8:00 p.m. Sat & Sun.
This is the busier of the two borders and is on the Pan-American Highway. Most expats who live in Guanacaste use this border crossing.

Los Chiles: 8:00 a.m. to 4:00 p.m.
Most expats who live in La Fortuna use this border crossing. It used to be a boat crossing, but now there's a road.

Nicaragua Border Fees

Leaving Costa Rica

- $7 Costa Rica Exit Fee (keep that receipt handy)
- $1 Nicaragua Municipal Tax
- $12 Nicaragua Entry Fee

Car Fees

- $1 Fumigation Fee

Returning to Costa Rica

- $1 Nicaragua Municipality Tax
- $2 Nicaragua Exit Fee
- No Costa Rica Entry Fee

Border Run Checklist

- ☐ Know the border hours, and be aware they may close for lunch. Remember, Panama is one hour ahead.
- ☐ Have a few pens handy.
- ☐ Bring US dollars. Make sure they are small bills. Panama and Nicaragua will not accept colones.
- ☐ When paying Costa Rica's exit fee, keep the receipt handy. Multiple people will ask to see it.
- ☐ Proof of Onward Travel: Costa Rica is now requesting proof of onward travel back to the country that issued your passport. A bus ticket will not suffice anymore. You will need a printed plane ticket when leaving Costa Rica.

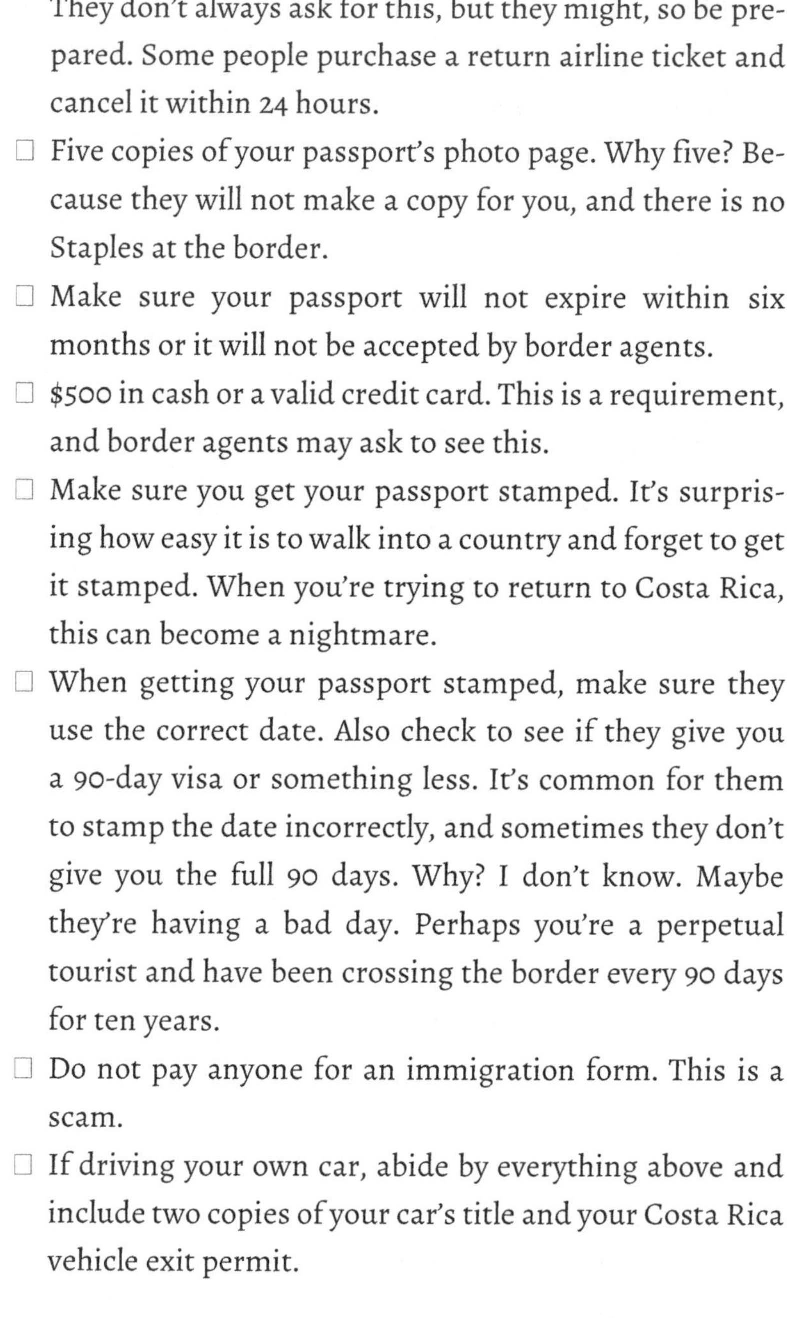

They don't always ask for this, but they might, so be prepared. Some people purchase a return airline ticket and cancel it within 24 hours.

- [ ] Five copies of your passport's photo page. Why five? Because they will not make a copy for you, and there is no Staples at the border.
- [ ] Make sure your passport will not expire within six months or it will not be accepted by border agents.
- [ ] $500 in cash or a valid credit card. This is a requirement, and border agents may ask to see this.
- [ ] Make sure you get your passport stamped. It's surprising how easy it is to walk into a country and forget to get it stamped. When you're trying to return to Costa Rica, this can become a nightmare.
- [ ] When getting your passport stamped, make sure they use the correct date. Also check to see if they give you a 90-day visa or something less. It's common for them to stamp the date incorrectly, and sometimes they don't give you the full 90 days. Why? I don't know. Maybe they're having a bad day. Perhaps you're a perpetual tourist and have been crossing the border every 90 days for ten years.
- [ ] Do not pay anyone for an immigration form. This is a scam.
- [ ] If driving your own car, abide by everything above and include two copies of your car's title and your Costa Rica vehicle exit permit.

Healthcare

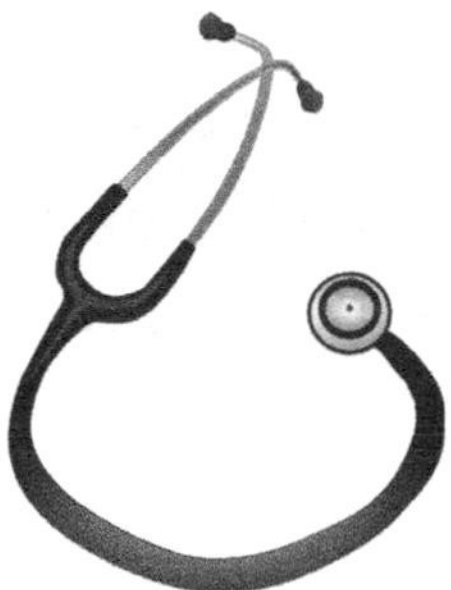

"My doctor gave me two weeks to live. I hope they're in August."

~ Ronnie Shakes

In *Happier Than A Billionaire: The Sequel,* I chronicled my husband's hernia surgery in a public hospital. It was a fine story, one that included me crying, Rob's stoicism, and the absence of any and all toilet seats. When I tell this story, everyone interrupts me after I mention the latter. It's too odd of a detail not to elaborate upon.

For some reason, there were absolutely no toilet seats in any restroom at Nicoya Hospital. It makes one question why? Is there a notorious toilet seat gang roaming the streets? And more importantly, how can I get in on the action?

I have never found an answer to this. I can only imagine that they were made of ice. But of all the things that could go wrong with the surgery, this small feature bothered Rob the most.

"I'm not going to the bathroom," he said.

"You're here for four days. That's not your best plan."

But Rob wasn't kidding; his best plan would involve not having a bowel movement in Nicoya Hospital. And he succeeded—a badge of honor he wears alongside his hernia scar. As for the surgery? It went well. Hercules recovered and went back to lifting things that are too heavy.

Pick up *Happier Than A Billionaire: The Sequel*—or as some reviewers like to call it, "Not as Good as the First"—if you want to read more about the magical story of when Rob underwent hernia surgery in Costa Rica. It's also when we had our license plate stolen off our car.

Caja and Public Hospitals

Costarricense de Seguro Social (C.C.S.S.) The good thing about health care is that all residents have it. We contribute to the C.C.S.S., known as Caja (caha), which is confusing because in Spanish that also means checkout, register, box, and slush funds.

I know people who have used Caja hospitals with great success. Some even had heart attacks and lived to tell about it. But there are some notable differences, and no toilet seats are just the start.

When using the Caja system, you first need to go to your locally assigned primary health care provider. That doctor will determine if your issue requires additional diagnostics and will send you to the appropriate facility. Our local provider is in a small building surrounded by barbed wire. When Rob blew out his hernia, we had to stand in line at six in the morning and didn't get seen for hours. The doctor will only examine a limited number of people, so you may have to come back several times before being seen. Eventually, the doctor saw us, and with one look at Rob's bulging intestines, he was referred to a surgeon at Nicoya Hospital.

A week before the surgery, we sat in a lecture with many other people waiting for surgery. The nurse gave instructions about different procedures and how to avoid infections, then demonstrated a catheter going into a man's penis. Not an actual penis, just an invisible one she was holding in the air, which coincidentally is exactly how I like to pantomime catheter insertions. The women laughed, but the men's eyes all but popped out of their heads. After the lecture, we received a piece of paper signed by the nurse. It reminded me of a hall pass.

This collective lecture saved valuable time. By getting everyone together at once, the doctor did not have to repeat this information to all of his patients. Not a bad idea when you think about it.

There are limited resources, so you must have a real problem to be admitted to the hospital. Do you have a little pain in your knee? It may take a while to get an MRI. But if your knee just got smashed in an accident, you'll be seen immediately, like the guy in the hospital bed next to Rob. He got into a motorcycle accident and broke every bone in his leg. He had many female visitors, and my husband casually mentioned that to one of the women, who just so happened to be the man's wife. I'm pretty she sure broke his other leg when he returned home.

If you are not a resident and have an emergency, you can still go to the public hospital. Few people speak English, so be prepared. You will also be charged.

The Caja Cost Your monthly premium during temporary residency will be higher than when you become a permanent resident. Premiums are calculated for temporary residents based on your pension or unearned income, previously discussed in my residency chapter. It's calculated as follows:

From $323 to $1011	5.18%
From $1011 to $2,023	6.24%
From $2023 to $3035	8.02%
Above $3035	10.69%

For example, if claiming $1011 as your monthly income for residency, you will pay $52 per month towards Caja.

Once you become a permanent resident, your monthly fee will be calculated the same, with the exception of a cap limiting the maximum amount.

Many expats have both Caja and a form of private health insurance that they purchase through INS (National Insurance Agency of Costa Rica).

Public Hospitals If you plan on becoming a resident, the following are some of the best-equipped public hospitals in the country:

- Hospital Nacional de Niño in San José: This is the best hospital for children in Costa Rica.
- Hospital San Juan de Dios in San José: They have a superb cardiac care department. They also treat burns and mental health issues.
- Hospital Rafael Ángel Calderón Guardi in San José
- Hospital Nacional Max Peralta Jimenez in Cartago
- Hospital Mexico in La Uruca

Private Healthcare

If you are not a resident, or if you choose not to go through Caja for any particular procedure, there are private hospitals throughout Costa Rica. They are more affordable when compared to prices in the United States. For example, I had a colonoscopy in a private hospital (El Hospital San Rafael Arcángel in Liberia) and it only cost $300. There were toilet seats galore! I enjoyed a little me time without having to balance like a hoverboard over the commode.

It just occurred to me that I'm blathering, something I promised I wouldn't do at the beginning of this book. I'm sorry, I can't help myself. But if you want to hear more about my funny colonoscopy experience, which many have said was my finest writing to date, you can find that story in the 2016 edition of *The Costa Rica Escape Manual.*

Rob recently went to El Hospital San Rafael Arcángel for an ultrasound. It cost $70, which included an initial consultation and an immediate and thorough review of exam findings. The technician even provided us with pictures to take back to our doctor. It was all fast and efficient.

Private hospitals take a few types of insurance. INS has medical plans that will cover you at these private facilities. Some may even accept your Blue Cross Blue Shield plan, but even if you don't have insurance, most times the cost of care is very reasonable.

Additional private insurance varies with age. For example, a person in their forties can expect to pay an annual premium of $2500 with a $10,000 deductible. Contact INS to get an accurate quote. Plans may even cover emergencies while visiting the United States for less than 45 days. There's a lot of small print, so it's important to take your time when reading over your contract.

Private Hospitals: If you choose to go to a private hospital, the following are some of the best in the country:

- CIMA hospital | www.hospitalcima.com | This facility is affiliated with Baylor University Medical Center in Dallas, Texas, and has state-of-the-art equipment. They are known as one of the best hospitals in the country, having an excellent coronary heart facility and diagnostic imaging center. Many people have orthopedic operations performed here. I know someone who had her baby at this hospital and raved about the care.
- Clínica Bíblica | www.clinicabiblica.com | This facility is affiliated with Evergreen Hospital in Kirkland, Washington. Their facilities are top-notch and popular with medical tourists.

- Clínica Católica | www.hospitallacatolica.com | This facility provides emergency care, nutritional counseling, psychiatric care, cardiology services, and respiratory treatments.
- El Hospital San Rafael Arcángel | www.hcsanrafael.com This is a great hospital in Liberia. They have many specialists and perform a variety of surgeries (general, bariatric, gynecological, laparoscopic, ophthalmologic, orthopedic, pediatric, plastic, and vascular).

Links:

Public Hospitals: http://www.ccss.sa.cr/hospitales
CAJA: http://www.ccss.sa.cr
INS of Costa Rica: www.ins-cr.com

Flamingo

Dental Tourism

"Dream of butterflies and waterfalls."
~ My Dentist

"Dream of butterflies and waterfalls," he said. I closed my eyes and imagined both. A waterfall plummeting into a pool surrounded by iridescent blue butterflies.

"Now think of lemonade. Not sweet but tart. A glass of tart lemonade," he continued. If you enjoy a little story time while getting your teeth cleaned, I have just the dentist for you.

Dr. Alan Alvarado is my adorable dentist. He has beautiful white teeth and incredible breath. These are essential qualities when someone is working so close to your face. And his pleasant stories are just another reason to visit him for your dental care.

After moving to Costa Rica, you'll quickly notice that most expats' mouths resemble an advertisement for Crest toothpaste. No matter the age, they have a beautiful smile, every single tooth standing at attention as if waiting to salute.

Costa Rica is known as the premier tourist destination for dental care. It's less expensive, and very similar to the United States. Dr. Alvarado's facility is no exception. His patients love him for his great work and kind demeanor. But don't take my word for it; there are others who share my view.

Ben and Michelle came to Costa Rica and stayed at The Happier House specifically for Dr. Alvarado's services. They read about him in *The Costa Rica Escape Manual* and decided that this was the option that best suited their budget. I asked Michelle if she could tell me about her and Ben's experience with Dr. Alvarado, and she was excited to share her story.

"We first decided to explore Costa Rica as an option for dental care when the area of Mexico where we had initially planned to visit became too dangerous for tourists. We had heard Costa Rica was a beautiful place to visit and after some research found that the cost of dental work was very affordable.

"Our initial concerns before making our appointment were that the dentist was highly recommended, professional, experienced, and their office was clean. We also needed an English-speaking dentist or a translator, as neither of us spoke Spanish. We found Dr. Alan Alvarado, and he met all of our expectations. He was an experienced dentist recommended in *The Costa Rica Escape Manual*, with a clean office and professional staff. He also spoke perfect English.

"My husband and I contacted him via email, as when you call the office, his Spanish-speaking assistant answers the phone. He emailed back within a day or two and responded to my questions regarding services and their general price range. We arranged a series of appointments during the time frame that fit our travel dates. We booked our dates about a month in advance.

"Ben and I had no trouble finding the office, thanks to a set of detailed instructions from our hostess. It's important to note that there are no proper addresses in Costa Rica, so landmarks are important. This was a surprise to us when we first arrived, but in no time we were zipping about and exploring in our rental car!!

"There were no other clients scheduled during our visits, so we were given the utmost care and attention. Everything was handled efficiently. We had an initial appointment where my husband received X-rays and a deep cleaning. I had X-rays and four out of nine cavities filled. It's a good idea to email Dr. Alvarado copies of your latest X-rays beforehand, so he is fully prepared for your visit.

"On our next visit, several days later, my husband had his top wisdom teeth pulled, and I had my other five cavities filled. On our third visit, I had my top wisdom teeth removed, and the fourth visit was a check-up for both of us. These four visits ranged over a total of twelve days. In our situation, our bill came in under $1000. This would have cost $5,000 in Tennessee.

"We felt that Dr. Alvarado's care was wonderful and very similar to the attention that we would have received in the United States. But we preferred Dr. Alvarado since he did our cleaning, exam, X-rays, and treatment all himself. We were given very close attention rather than being shuffled around in a big, busy office."

Dr. Alvarado works with an oral surgeon, so his office can handle not only common cosmetic dental procedures but more complicated cases as well. Or you can just see him for a cleaning; he'll whisper a lovely fairytale while scraping plaque off your teeth. And we could all use a little lemonade and waterfalls while reclining in a dentist's chair.

Dr. Alan Alvarado
Huacas, Guanacaste
Phone: (506) 2653-8308
Fax: (506) 2653-8308
www.costadental.com
email: costadental1@gmail.com

Working in Costa Rica

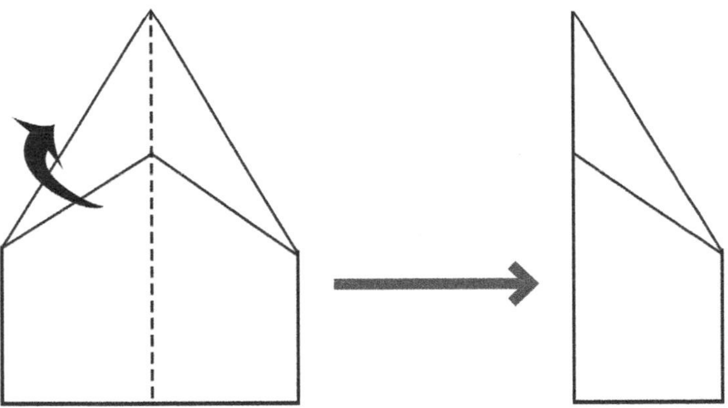

Fold at crease

Can I Work Legally?

"I just want to lie on the beach and eat hot dogs. That's all I've ever wanted."

~ Kevin Malone
The Office

Many people move to Costa Rica first and then search for employment. What they soon discover is that they cannot work legally without permanent residency. It's a big kink in their hard-and-fast escape plan. But there are two exceptions, and one may be your ticket to paradise: obtaining a work permit or opening a business. Both have their challenges, and things are not always as easy as they appear.

Work Permit

Do you have a skill set that an employer can't find locally? If so, you may be able to obtain a work permit. This permit, although not a form of residency, allows you to live in Costa Rica as long as you are working at that particular job. I should mention that salaries are much less than what you might make for the same job in other countries.

This applicant must be approved by two governmental agencies, the Department of Immigration and the Ministry of Labor. That's one government agency too many in my book. Have you ever tried applying for Caja (the pubic healthcare system), at the Caja building, in front of the Caja clerk, with all your Caja papers? There are one million things that can go wrong. So I can't even imagine how long two government agencies can hold up a work permit.

But now I *can* imagine it, because I've asked someone who knows. It can take over a year, and if you're going to give it a try, it's in your best interest to hire an attorney to help you with the paperwork. The employer is responsible for filing your application to the Department of Immigration, and most are reluctant to do so. Aside from the paperwork involved, it costs them a significant amount of money.

Once again, I contacted Marcia Solis, our residency expert at Send Me South, to weigh in on the chances of an expat obtaining a work permit.

"I wouldn't suggest anyone going this route," she says. "It is a frustrating process, and applicants must comply with everything the government requires. A better scenario is when someone comes hired by a company that has already gone through its enrollment process at Immigration."

That last statement is crucial. If you are inquiring about an advertised position, ask the company if they have already gone through its enrollment process. This will save you time and money.

Employer's Work Permit Checklist

- ☐ Letter describing the exact activity their prospective employee will perform and the reason they require that specific skill set.
- ☐ Financial statements showing they have the means to pay the prospective employee and are in good standing with the Costa Rican social security system.
- ☐ Proof that they are up to date with taxes, insurance, and corporate registration documents.

Employee's Work Permit Checklist

- ☐ Letter of Intent, addressed to the General Direction of Immigration, with name, nationality, address, intended occupation, passport number, and the amount of time the applicant will be living in Costa Rica. This document must be notarized in Costa Rica.
- ☐ A certified birth certificate authenticated by the Costa Rican consulate of the employee's country, and a police report from the town the employee resides in. These documents must be apostilled in the country in which they originated and then translated into Spanish by an official translator registered at the Ministry of Foreign Affairs of Costa Rica.

- ☐ Diplomas or degrees related to employment. They must be apostilled in the country where they originated.
- ☐ A certified copy of every page of the employee's passport.
- ☐ Fingerprinted at the Ministry of Public Security in Costa Rica. The record must be attached to the application upon filing.
- ☐ A deposit of $200 into a specific government bank account. The receipt for this must be presented to Immigration.

Opening a Business

"We'll open a low-rider classic car shop!" Jim tells Hazel.

This sounds like a swell plan. Everyone enjoys a brain stem injury after hitting one of those colossal Costa Rican potholes. Your idea is stupid, Jim. So before you import your 1977 Chevrolet Monte Carlo, let's first discuss Article 80 of the Immigration Law:

"The Temporary Resident may only carry out remunerated work or lucrative self-employed activities which have been authorized by the Department of Immigration. The Department will evaluate the recommendations of the Ministry of Labor and other criteria of convenience and opportunity in conferring any authorization."

What does this mean, Hazel? Your guess is as good as mine. But I am certain that, if you own a restaurant, you should not be waiting on tables. And if Jim plans on altering his Monte Carlo's suspension, he better plan on hiring a Costa Rican to do it. You cannot perform any job that can be filled by a Costa Rican citizen.

For example, at The Happier House, I can make your bed and wash your towels. I'll even delicately fold the first toilet paper sheet into a rose for you and Jim. He loves that. I can do this because I'm a permanent resident. If I wasn't, I could only watch someone do it.

What happens if a temporary resident gets caught breaking this rule? Some have been escorted to the airport and kicked out of the country. Others have sat at Immigration under a blinding light and been interrogated. Okay, I made up the blinding light part. Ticos are pretty laid-back, and I'm sure they'll offer you coffee before leaving you in the hot seat while they enjoy an extended lunch break. But you are in trouble, Jim. There's no doubt about it.

The next question probably floating around in your mind is what type of business you should open. We live in a tourist area, so that creates many opportunities. If you lived in the mountains, you might want to cater to the local population. Understanding the dynamics of where you live is key to starting up a viable business. Sometimes that means living in the area for six months or more.

Hiring Employees

Tim and Kim are a married couple that own Beach Treats Homemade Ice Cream Bolas and Loco Mini Golf in Tamarindo. They shared with me information about the taxes and their considerations when hiring employees.

- 9.3% of each employee's salary needs to be paid in toward Caja, to cover social security and health care benefits.

- An additional 25% comes out of the employer's pocket toward Caja.
- The employer must contribute toward workers' compensation, a charge that's determined by the employees' occupation. My employees are categorized as cashiers, but if they were construction workers or armed security guards, their workers' compensation fees would be much higher.
- Vacation pay is mandatory. Employees get a two-week paid vacation after working one full year. There's also a bonus that employees receive called an *aquinaldo*, which can be calculated by taking the worker's salary over one year (from December 1 to December 1) and dividing it by twelve.
- Termination of employees can be challenging. If an employee has worked less than 90 days, you can fire them for any reason. However, you will still need to pay a prorated portion of their vacation pay and *aquinaldo*. After 90 days, it becomes even more complicated. We recently needed to let someone go and thought we only had to pay her vacation and *aquinaldo*. But she fought us, and in the end we had to give her severance pay as well. I would suggest business owners present employees with written warnings that they must sign when they are not performing their job properly. After several infractions, you'll have a record of your employee's job performance. This is important information if your worker should fight you in court for severance.

I've seen successes and failures. Sometimes it's an idea that was doomed from the start. Other times it's just an irresponsible owner. Starting a business is challenging in any country. Now imagine starting one in a foreign environment, with different rules, no addresses, and possibly in a language you still haven't mastered. You'll be starting from behind the eight ball. But that doesn't mean you shouldn't chalk your cue stick and go for the shot.

There are plenty of people making a living in Costa Rica, but it will take passion, endurance and specifically thrust (the third of our paper airplane aeronautical concepts). Thrust is a force and is used to describe how strongly an object is pushed. And you are going to need thrust, a whole bunch of it to get where you're going. On days when you don't have any, you'll need someone else to give you a shove. Often, it's the last nudge that gets you through the fiercest winds.

Opening a business is achievable in Costa Rica, and the next chapters are about people doing just that—tossing caution to the wind and following a dream. They may just inspire you to do the same.

Links:

Marcia Solis at Send Me South : www.sendmesouth.com
Immigration: www.migracion.go.cr
Beach Treats Homemade Ice Cream:
www.facebook.com/BeachTreatsCR

Going With the Flō

"You are the sky, everything else is just the weather."
~ Pema Chodron

There are two types of videos I like watching on Instagram: goats in pajamas, and the videos on Stephanie Gongora's Yoga Page (@Casa_Colibri). And I'm not alone—she has close to half a million followers watching too.

Her videos go viral because they're beautiful. She twirls in pretty white dresses or does handstands in the rain on her jungle platform. There is rarely one where Stephanie isn't upside down. She calls it movement therapy, and the name fits. It's therapeutic just watching her, even if I do so while drinking a cup of coffee on my couch, where I'm performing no movement at all.

It was surprising when I received a message notifying me that I had been tagged in one of her Instagram stories. Before she moved to Central America to build her retreat center, she and her husband, Ben, bought my books and read them out loud to each other. It's ironic since my entire first year in Costa Rica, I felt as if my life had been turned upside down. There was a lot of movement therapy in that first book. I was never happier.

Stephanie and Ben did something big. They didn't open a restaurant, or even a bed-and-breakfast. They built a sprawling retreat center in the middle of the Uvita jungle project—so ambitious that I had to reach out to her for this book.

"How did you meet your husband?" I ask.

"We were both doing medical work in Nicaragua while in college. I did not like him then. He was a baseball player, very much a jock. The trip changed his perspective. It was towards the end of college when I fell in love with him.

"I always wanted to move to either Mexico or Central America. I'm half Mexican and visited my family in Chihuahua, Mexico every year. After spending those semesters in Nicaragua, I knew I wanted to move there and open a business. I wasn't sure what it would be, but I tucked that dream in the back of my head."

"If Nicaragua was on your radar, why did you choose Costa Rica?"

"Before Ben and I got married, we came down to Costa Rica and loved it. We returned every year and decided that if we were going to run a business, Costa Rica might be a better option than Nicaragua. Costa Rica had a smoother—not smooth, but smoother—path to residency, better marketing potential, and overall it was a better fit for us.

"I love the Hispanic culture, hot weather, greenery, and tiny towns. Ben and I wanted a place where we could live the things we think are important. We're both in the wellness field, and I believe getting out of an urban environment makes a big difference in your health and fitness. We wanted other people to experience all of that through our retreat.

"The very first time we came down, we stayed in Uvita, a small but functional beach town. We went home, and I discovered your first book and started reading. I was excited to learn about a normal couple taking on hardships with humor and patience.

"Our dream took shape, and we toured real estate for five years. We kept coming back to Uvita because we loved it so much. I know we probably should have looked around more, but we didn't. We walked into a real estate office, something I wouldn't recommend doing, but we got lucky and found a great realtor who had such patience with us. He took us down back roads that we would never have found on our own.

"Our first property didn't pan out, so we tried a second one, and at the last second, the seller doubled his price. The third time led us to the property we own now. I was drawn to the fact it is twenty acres, with seven waterfalls, and tons of privacy.

"We built our house first, then our retreat center. The scariest time was when we started running out of money, so we began advertising before the retreat was completed! We asked our construction crew if it was possible to finish on time. They said yes, so we promoted our first retreat and yoga training seminar for March 2018. And with that money, we finished construction the day of the first retreat."

"How did the construction process go for you and Ben?" I ask.

"We were lucky, and things went well. Oh, except for the fire and flood. Yep. That was a hiccup." Only a yoga instructor could be nonchalant discussing a fire and flood.

"A combination of special lights in wooden holders and an electrical surge caused the fire. It burned down half the roof. Then, last rainy season, we had seven straight days of monsoon-like rain, and it flooded our house. But Ben and I got through it together."

"Were there any water permit issues? I know that Costa Rica is making laws stricter."

"Getting a concession for water is a very important step. It used to be once you applied for a concession in our zone and turned in your documents, you could start building. That's what we did. Then the law changed, stating you had to get concessions first before beginning construction. That can take years and will drastically change a developer's timeline. Luckily, we were grandfathered in. But that could have changed everything for us. Many people try to get water illegally. That's a horrible idea and I would not recommend anyone doing that."

"Ben, you handled the construction process. Do you have any advice for someone wanting to follow in your footsteps?"

"Costa Rica is all about persistence and perseverance," he says. "If that will get you down in any way, if you are not someone who will jump through twenty hurdles, this place is not for you.

"It's important to have weekly and monthly goals. I made sure the crew had what they needed. They worry about problems once they arise, while I plan for them before they happen."

"Do you have any advice for someone considering moving here and starting a business?"

"Everything is more complicated, and much slower, which is fine for me," Stephanie adds. "I'm more like your husband. I can roll with it. Like my quest for registering for Caja. I have to be enrolled before I can go to Immigration and get my cédula. Ben has already been accepted to Caja, so now I can apply as his dependent. But my last name is different, so they didn't want to add me to his policy. After straightening that out, they said Ben just has to show up and do the paperwork, but when he went to the office, they decided I needed to be there as well. I went there today, but it's closed. It's not even a holiday. I'll have to go back and try a third time to get into the system.

"So today, instead of sitting in the Caja office, we drove to the Panama border. A company sent me a drum for my retreat, and it got stopped at customs. Since it was in my name, I was the only one who could pick it up unless I prepared a signed and notarized letter allowing someone else to do it. We drove two and a half hours to the border, stopped at one customs office to pay for storage of the package, another to verify the payment, and then one where they charged me for something else. I don't even know what for. This process took three hours. Not including the driving."

"On that note, is there anything you wish you had here? What could make things easier?"

"I wish I had a better car," Stephanie laughs. "You think differently about vehicles in Costa Rica. They are expensive, so we own a 2000 Nissan Xterra with 100,000 miles. We've had it for two years, and it breaks down all the time. It stalls and shuts off completely when I make a turn. Ben thinks that's no big deal, and just tells me to use the emergency brakes when it happens."

Apparently, Ben and my husband are on the same page when it comes to driving junky old cars.

"Oh, there is also a gas leak. Ben thinks that isn't a big deal either. 'Don't fill up the tank more than half-way,' he tells me. That's his solution."

"Flō Retreat Center sounds incredible. Could you tell me more about it?"

"Our retreat is a rental space for events centered on health and wellness. Anything from yoga, meditation, and nutrition. We are not a hotel or hostel. We are available for five or more nights, and you can rent either the main building or the whole center. The main building can sleep sixteen people, and you have access to our top-of-the-line gym and yoga studio. We also have cabinas in the forest for more lodging accommodations.

"Ben offers both beginner retreats and continuing education seminars on wellness and fitness for doctors, trainers, and health and movement professions. I offer teacher training, retreats, and intensives.

"We believe that health is not worrying about your health. A big part of being healthy is environment and stress levels. Do you get fresh air and sunlight, and is your food clean? Are you enjoying yourself during the day?

"Flō is an oasis, where people can learn and grow, whether that be through meditation, nutrition, movement, yoga, dance, or aerial therapy. When you remove yourself from your everyday life to a place close to nature, you quickly adopt a healthier way of living. You'll even experience a more natural sleeping cycle. People are surprised when they fall asleep by nine p.m. and wake up with the howler monkeys at five a.m. Removing yourself from your current environment, even for a week, can help you adopt little patterns you can take home and apply to your everyday life."

I like this couple, one that is pursuing a dream and sharing their philosophy with the world. They complement each other, Stephanie with her graceful movements and Ben bench-pressing very heavy things. Check out his Instagram page, where he lifts over three hundred pounds. I watch his videos too while lifting my coffee mug, which isn't heavy at all.

But like Stephanie stated, you come to Costa Rica to bask in the environment. So I'm getting off this couch and going for a walk. My movement therapy will be hiking to the top of a mountain, where I'll stare out at the ocean. I won't do any handstands or swirl around in a pretty dress, but I'll be happy and grateful that my aching legs, the air in my lungs, and the blood in my heart got me there.

And then I will lift a rock. Just for Ben.

Links:

Flō Retreat Center: www.floretreatcenter.com
Stephanie's Instagram Page:
www.instagram.com/casa_colibri
Ben's Instagram Page:
www.instagram.com/drbenhouse

Children's Bookstore

"A book is a dream that you hold in your hand."
~ Neil Gaiman

I found the real Meg Ryan from *You've Got Mail.* She owns an adorable children's bookstore and is an equally adorable owner—Kimberly Turner of Page Turner Books.

I walk inside her shop and find Kimberly, her blond hair pulled back into a ponytail, moving a box of books into a storage room. Her store has that wonderful book smell. It may be the most pleasant in all the world. It makes me want to sit in a tiny chair and read *I'll Love You to the Moon and Back.*

As I walk around, I notice that the scale of this store matches the scale of me. There are tiny shopping carts and a little table with little chairs in the corner. I feel right at home.

Kimberly came to Costa Rica with a husband and two small children in tow. He was offered a position with a development company, so I assumed he had to convince her on the move.

"Absolutely not. If anyone was pushing the conversation, it was me. I was a stay-at-home mom and I'll be honest, I was bored. I wanted an adventure, and Costa Rica sounded awesome."

I'm surprised by her honesty. This is the exact situation that would discourage most people from moving, but she saw a different life for herself. That familiar spark all expats have in common.

After a few years, her husband's position ended, and they needed to formulate a new plan. "We realized that we had nothing keeping us here, and nothing making us go back. We took many walks on the beach to discuss what we both really wanted. What we thought home would look like. And it turns out it looked like right here.

"My daughter takes dance lessons in this building, and I'd walk the halls and look at the empty storefronts. I'd imagine what each space would look like, what kind of store it could be, and then it hit me. I saw the image of a children's bookstore. It was a complete picture. I saw every bookshelf: piñatas hanging from the ceiling; stuffed animals along the periphery. It was all right in front of me! I knew what I wanted to do, but then I had to figure out how to make that happen."

"Did you have any experience in retail? People say don't come here and start something new. It's better to do something you know a lot about."

"Yeah, I didn't do that. In fact, I did the opposite. I knew nothing about running a store, inventory, or shipping items. Nothing! Every step of this was new to me."

With no experience, Kim dove straight into opening her shop. She laboriously hand-scraped a layer of glue off the floor, for weeks, without air conditioning because she didn't yet have the business license one needs to obtain an electric meter. This is a corner store, on the second floor, surrounded by windows. It must have been scorching. The true definition of sweat equity.

"There were so many things that needed to get done. Applying for permits, setting up utilities, and finding distributors. Every part of it was new to me. And I loved it all."

"Is there anything you learned along the way about running a store," I ask, "that may differ from in the States?"

"One of my biggest blunders was not timing our shipments correctly. I thought placing an order six weeks out was sufficient. No, it's not. I found that out when my Christmas shipment arrived in January. And just in case I needed to experience that again, the same thing occurred for my Easter shipment. Now I order over two months ahead.

"Another thing, which many in Costa Rica know but seems absurd to anyone else, is that there are no proper addresses. You basically make one up. My first address was the name of this shopping center, but some of my deliveries never arrived, so I made up a new one. Now my address states I'm in the old ICE (phone company) building. Everyone who lives in Brasilito remembers the phone company used to have an office here, but how would anyone new to the area know that? It's one of those Costa Rica riddles you just have to live with."

"What is your advice to people thinking of opening a business in Costa Rica?"

"My advice is to be flexible. Ask for help when you need it. Hire good employees since they make all the difference. Whenever I ran into obstacles, my employees helped with all the nuts and bolts."

Kim is planning on expanding her inventory into science kits and other products for older children. She is constantly thinking a week, a month, and six months ahead. Running her business takes up much of her time and raising a family fills up the rest. But Kimberly does it with a shake of her ponytail, and with resolve knowing that she's living life on her terms, doing exactly what she wants to do.

"All of us expats, we see life like a lottery," she says. "Some tickets we win, some we lose, but we just keep on going."

Page Turner Books
Paseo Del Mar Building
Huacas, Guanacaste
Email: pageturnerbookscr@gmail.com
www.facebook.com/Pageturnerbooks

Beer at the Beach

"Imagine lemonade, sitting poolside," Cathy says. I sip the beer and close my eyes, remembering hot summer days with my sister in New Jersey. The coolness of the beer sinks all the way down to my toes.

It's noon, and I'm already having the perfect day at Cerveceria Independiente brewery, sitting at a picnic table and recalling some childhood memories. We're only two blocks from the Pacific Ocean, and I smell lazy salty breezes blowing in my direction. At noon, Costa Rican breezes are always lazy, reminding everyone it's siesta time. I open my eyes and Cathy hands me another sample to taste. If you like craft beer and friendly business owners, this should be your first stop on your next vacation.

Behind me stands a two-story display window with large silver brew kettles lined up neatly in a row. I drink my beer in the sunshine while Cathy's husband goes back and forth, turning knobs and taking notes. He's wearing a conical straw hat like a farmer in a rice paddy. It makes me smile.

"Yeah, he likes that hat. He always wears it," she laughs. I notice the way she looks at him. It's the same way I look at Rob. It's a sparkle that reveals you still like your husband, even after years of marriage. I believe it's easier to love someone than to like them. *Like* means you can run a business together without it devolving into a mixed martial arts match. Not many couples can do it.

Expats have ideas of opening a business, but rarely do I see one this big. An actual brewery? I needed to learn more about this couple, and if it takes testing eight different beers to find out how it all started, well, I have the resolve to see it through.

Before breweries or even Costa Rica was on their radar, Cathy and her husband were adventure guides in South America. But not any kind of guides. They were the ones that took you to the end of the road, and then went farther, and then continued a bit more after that. These trips were for the adventurers of the world, those who would rather sleep in a tent on a mountaintop than stay at a Four Seasons in Miami.

After two years of traveling throughout South America, they decided to work the ski season in Utah. Their life was always about adventure, and it's the foundation of their relationship. After getting married, they started a family and TJ began brewing beer in his garage. Every weekend, friends would stop by and taste test his newest recipe. It began as a fun hobby but turned into something he was more passionate about doing than anything else. During this time, Cathy worked for a marketing company and became restless at her job.

"It was soul-crushing," she says. Cathy didn't need to elaborate. I knew all too well about leaving a job that didn't seem to fit. "I wanted another adventure, and it was then we headed to Costa Rica. While I was pregnant with my second child!"

"But that seems crazy. Did you know anything about Costa Rica?"

"No, but it didn't sound crazy because that's the life we led. It's just who we are. When we see an adventure, we take it. We packed up, moved down, and had our second child in Costa Rica."

Cathy took another marketing job that enabled her to work remotely while her husband rented a small room above a restaurant and turned it into a beer laboratory. He tested flavors and worked on consistency, with the ultimate goal of making the best beer in Costa Rica. Besides a few howler monkey break-ins (he learned that monkeys love grain, and not to leave the windows open), he started making progress. He shared his product with friends he knew would be honest with him. He got a lot of comments like, "Not digging it," before it became "It's okay," to finally, "Can I buy a case of this?" That's when Cathy and TJ knew they had to see this dream to fruition. What they embarked on would be quite the challenge in any country.

"Did you have any clue where to start?" I ask.

"No. We knew nothing about opening a business in Costa Rica, let alone one as involved as this."

They found the right piece of property, a spot close to the beach, and began the buildout. They wanted the tanks in a front display window, so people immediately knew it was a brewery.

"Everything took longer than we expected. All the equipment had to be imported, and we had to keep being flexible with our construction."

"Was there something that surprised you? Something that wouldn't have happened in the States?"

"It was frustrating because they didn't know how to permit us! They just couldn't figure it out, so we have all these permits hanging on the wall for everything from serving food to distributing alcohol. We're covered for a lot of things."

A tourist approaches, and Cathy excuses herself. I walk around to the adjacent lot and see a large mural painted on the wall. Men are cutting into storage containers while others are laying concrete block.

"We are building a beer garden," Cathy says after serving her customer. "Those storage containers will be food vendors. Easy, handheld items. We're committed to less waste, especially less plastic." She then points to the men stacking concrete blocks. "They're building a Yakatori grill, and behind that will be a stage for live music. In the back corner will be a children's area. We want it to be a community gathering spot, where everyone can come together in a happy, relaxed place. Hey, would you like a root beer float?"

Is this lady my fairy godmother? "Of course," I tell Cathy. She disappears and returns with one of the most delicious floats. Cathy makes her own ice cream and has added this to their menu.

"The kids love them," she says, "and I'm expanding into other nonalcoholic beverages like fizzy strawberry and pineapple drinks."

"What advice would you give to someone who wants to open a business here?"

"You need to work together. Each person has his or her own strengths. There will be obstacles, but it's important not to give up. We see so many people quitting because things get hard and they won't see it through. Work past the hard times. You have to lean on each other. If you need help, ask for it. And keep looking into the future. Both my husband and I see our beer being sold in restaurants all around the country. This is our ultimate goal."

"I'm happy for you. This is a great idea," I say while sipping the last drop of my root beer float.

"We make good beer, in hot weather, near the beach. And those three things are a great combination."

It's funny but true. They may have found the perfect mixture for a successful business. Cathy hands me another beer and tells me to close my eyes. This has been a fun day, with the perfect couple, at the coolest establishment only blocks from the sand.

Cerveceria Independiente

Potrero, Guanacaste

beer@independiente.cr

8464-0935

www.independiente.cr

The Happier House

Buying Property

Developing and/or Subdividing Land

Jim and Hazel see a large parcel of land for sale online in Costa Rica. They email the seller, who states that they can develop it any way they wish. The couple fly down, travel to the property on horseback, and instantly fall in love with the area. It's paradise, and ideas run through Jim's head. He can imagine a community here, with many houses. If he sold off a few lots, it would cover the cost of the entire purchase.

"There is a river on the property," the seller says. "That's your water source."

"There aren't any roads. Besides horseback, how will anyone get here?" Hazel asks.

"No problem. Just carve a road through the forest," he tells her.

Jim plucks a mango off a tree, and both he and his wife ride back to their hotel. The couple is buzzing with excitement, and Hazel pulls out *The Costa Rica Escape Manual* from her suitcase and thumbs to this chapter. After finishing it, they both realize that there's more to developing this property than the seller has let on. A whole lot more.

To get the correct information on this very complicated issue, I spoke with real estate expert Brett Berkowitz. With over twenty-five years of experience in Costa Rica, Brett served it to me straight, much like a tequila shot. Mixed with Tabasco sauce. Then set on fire.

How easy is it to subdivide land in Costa Rica?

"Less than one in ten will succeed. It's not for the faint of heart or for people without a lot of money. Do not underestimate the cost. No matter how much homework you do, it is a huge risk because there is no way of knowing whether you will get the entitlements you will need to complete your project."

What kind of due diligence would you suggest before closing on a property?

"It is reasonable to ask for three to six months of due diligence before closing on any property. Negotiate a deposit that may or may not be refundable. In return, the seller should take the listing off the market to give you time to investigate. You'll need an attorney versed in developing land, and it will be expensive."

If there is a river on the property, does that guarantee you a viable water source?

"One of the biggest challenges for any project is water. Where is it coming from? What is the quality? What is the quantity? You'll have to hire one of several reputable companies that use sophisticated electronics to determine if there is water in the ground and how deep you might need to dig. It will cost around five thousand dollars just to perform this study.

"Although there may be rivers and springs running through the land, all bodies of water belong to the state. Do not assume that you will be able to pull water out of these sources without permission. If you get caught doing so, you'll immediately be shut down."

When can I start building? Do I need approval from government agencies?

"You will need an environmental impact study that the state will either approve or disapprove. This includes a water, forestry, and environmental engineer. You will also need a hydrogeologist. This study will take three to six months just to prepare a preliminary report.

"It's good to do a preliminary report first because a full report can take up to a year and the seller will not keep the property off the market for that long. A full report can cost as much as fifty thousand dollars, so a preliminary report can save you from wasting money by finding a problem right away. This report should be at least one hundred pages, and it gets submitted to Setena (Secretaría Técnica Nacional Ambiental). They will either grant you the entitlements or deny them. If they are denied, you just spent a lot of money for nothing."

What if there are many trees on the property? If I own the property, can I clear the land?

"Every tree needs to be inventoried and must be presented as a forestry inventory report. This will be done by your forestry engineer and will determine if roads will be granted. In other words, Setena will need to know the location and type of every tree on your property. If there is an endangered tree where you need to put a road, you cannot cut it down. You must move the road or not have a road at all.

"If the land is considered *bosque* (forest), it is very hard to get the permits you will need. Forestry inventory is very important because most land is considered forest. If you cut down the wrong tree, you will do jail time and/or pay a huge fine.

"The forestry engineer also needs to check that the substrate is suitable for a road. A soil study, which costs several thousand dollars, must also be performed because certain substrates, like clay, are not good and will wash out."

What happens after I get my environmental impact study? Am I ready to move ahead with my project?

"If your environmental impact study is approved by Setena, you must make a huge financial deposit to ensure you will follow the environmental impact rules. This deposit will be hundreds of thousands of dollars.

"The commitment you have made to respect the environment will now be overseen be an environmental regent granted by Setena. He will keep a logbook and visit your property at least once per month to mitigate your impact on the environment. You will pay a fee to this regent of about one thousand dollars a month depending on the size of your project. If you do not follow the rules, you can lose your deposit."

Besides Setena, what other government agencies will I be working with?

"Once you have passed the Setena hurdle, it's time to start urban planning. This is done through INVU (Instituto Nacional de Vivienda y Urbanismo). Many factors come into play including the amount of water your wells can provide. They will approve an allowed density. This determines the number of homes, how tall they can be, and the type of roads you can cut.

"MINAE (Ministerio de Ambiente y Energía) will also inspect your property and look for named rivers and monitor how and where you will deposit trash, black water, gray water, and pluvial or rain water. In other words, all of this will need to be dealt with in a responsible manner that does not pollute any bodies of water. These rules are getting stricter every year."

Is it possible to find a parcel that has all of this preapproved?

"You can find a preapproved development with entitlements already granted to the current owner. This will put you up to three years ahead and save you the risk of losing hundreds of thousands of dollars. The only risk involved with this approach relates to the developer's desired density.

"For example, let's say the owner was given entitlements to build a nine-story building but the local rights have changed, only allowing three-story buildings in your township. The new owner will be limited to building three-story structures in accordance with the local rights."

What if you don't want to subdivide but want to build a home and rent a bunch of cabinas?

"For the person who wishes to develop one big property, but not subdivide it, the process is not as complicated. You will need to jump through many of the same hurdles, but you may be granted more leniency. The amount of water under the ground will determine how many cabinas you can build. You will still need a forestry study before cutting any roads. If the developer plans on building over five thousand square feet of construction, it becomes more complicated, and an entire environmental study must go through Setena, exactly as if you were subdividing property."

As you can see, the due diligence steps required will take you longer than the 3 to 6 months that a seller may grant, which is why developing any property in Costa Rica is high risk.

Real Estate Checklist

If your best friend is buying a piece of property in what looks like an established development in Costa Rica, what are the top five things he should look for?

- ☐ As in North America or any place on the planet, the most important thing will be location, location, location.
- ☐ Get a clean and legal title researched by a real estate attorney. The title can be checked online at the national

registry. If you do not speak Spanish, make sure your attorney is bilingual. He should be honest and service-oriented. You can rule out some attorneys by checking for complaints made to the Colegio de Abogados y Abogadas de Costa Rica. The information is in Spanish, so use a translator. Be careful when making complaints because libel laws are strict in Costa Rica.

- ☐ Quality, quantity, and legality of water. Ask for a water letter stamped and signed by a legal ASADA (Asociación Administradoras de los Sistemas de Acueductos y Alcantarillados), as well as the president of that ASADA. Do not take its legitimacy at face value. Have it checked by your attorney. Your attorney must contact AYA (Instituto Costarricense de Acueductos y Alcantarillados) to confirm that it is, in fact, a registered ASADA. This is done online. Your attorney must also obtain a personería. This is a printout from the registry that proves the president of the ASADA has the legal right to sign the water letter.
- ☐ Check the history of the location. Is it a gated development? If so, is the security trustworthy? You can check this by speaking with neighbors in the community in an effort to discover whether there have been break-ins or crime-related issues. If it's not a gated community, is it a guarded condo complex? What is the reputation of their guards? If neither applies, ask around and see what the locals have to say.
- ☐ Understand the climate and ask about amenities. Be sure to understand that the weather is very different around the country and varies from one season to an-

other. Will the area provide you with your dream life? What activities are available in the area? Do you golf, fish, play tennis, gamble, etc.? Will you be near lakes, rivers, the beach? Are there roads to your lot? If so, are they paved? Weather can wash out dirt roads in a single rainy season. It's smart to spend some time in Costa Rica during the rainy season to get an idea of how it affects the property you're considering.

Thinking about buying land and disappearing for a while? Don't do it. There is something called **Squatters' Rights**, and it means exactly what it sounds like. According to Costa Rican law, a person can acquire rights if the property owner allows that person to use or maintain possession of the property for more than a year. Once the property has been acquired, it cannot be taken away, except for reasons such as eminent domain, and then only with proper compensation.

Links:

Setena: www.setena.go.cr

INVU: www.invu.go.cr

MINAE: www.minae.go.cr

AYA: www.aya.go.cr

Colegio de Abogados y Abogadas de Costa Rica: www.abogados.or.cr

The Water Letter

"If my ship sails from sight, it doesn't mean my journey ends, it simply means the river bends."

~ Enoch Powell

It is imperative that water distribution to your home and/or project is legal. Brett, from the previous chapter, helped shed light on the various ways of obtaining legal water. And by legal, I mean that the developer has the right to deliver water to each parcel within the project. It's something that most people are not aware of before purchasing land, and it can be the difference between fulfilling your dream and losing your money.

Costa Rica is the legal owner of all water, and even mineral rights below the soil. Just because there is water on your property does not mean it's legal to use it. Even if PVC pipes are running to your lot and the seller says, "Look, just turn on the faucet, and you have running water!" that does not guarantee any of it is legal.

Different Concessions Granted to Access Water

Legally Registered Artesian Well (Hand-Dug) This type of concession is only meant for agricultural and uni-residential purposes. It's a legal water system for only one farmhouse on one farm. It is illegal for this landowner to distribute water to areas outside the boundaries of his farm or to multiple properties cut from the mother farm. Although legal, it's the least favorable concession.

It's not uncommon to come across a seller who has subdivided his land into smaller parcels and claims he can legally provide water to each lot. You need to check if the seller has the right not only to pump water from this well but also to distribute the water to others. Request this proof in writing, and have your attorney double-check the authenticity against the public records at AYA in San José.

If you buy an existing home with this water setup, there is some risk. If buying a piece of property with the intent of building on it, you are at extreme risk of never getting a building permit.

Neighborhood Usage Association A group of neighbors get together and have concession rights to one well (either artesian or machine-dug). This group is responsible for maintaining water quality and the infrastructure needed to distribute water. This type of association, while not the strongest form of water rights, is usually tolerated and grandfathered in if the neighborhood water association has been around for many years, and if there are no complaints generated about the quality of the system. Mature neighborhood associations are unlikely to be challenged by Costa Rica providing that their wells are legally registered, they have a legal concession granted to withdraw a preapproved quantity of water, and they stick to pumping that amount of water or less.

Condominium Water System In this case, a well is registered duly to the condominium for the administration and distribution of water. Costa Rica will require the well within the condominium property to be legally registered, and will also require that the condominium is granted a concession to withdraw water from that well. To be clear, the seller needs to provide two forms of documentation: one proves legal registration of the well, and the other proves there is a concession for the use of its water.

ASADA (The best scenario for water rights.) An ASADA (Asociación Administradora del Acueducto y Alcantarillado) is a community organization bound by strict rules governing the creation and administration of all registered wells and concessions within the limits of the infrastructure of that ASADA.

An ASADA may or may not be entered into a Convenio de Delegación (which means a delegation contract with the National Water Association). Either way, an ASADA is a strong form of water rights. However, one that has entered into a Convenio de Delegación is the most desirable, as this is the most solid form of water rights a property can have in Costa Rica.

An ASADA must also be duly registered. ASADAs that have entered into a Convenio de Delegación have the full and legal right to substitute for the National Water Association as it relates to all matters concerning water generation and distribution for a community. It is the most solid form of water rights a property can have within Costa Rica. This is the water system we have in our community, Mar Vista.

What water documents do I need to obtain a building permit for a home?

You must provide two essential water documents before you are given a building permit from your local municipality. The first document is what is referred to as a Water Availability Letter. This letter is a prerequirement of the municipality before they will even consider granting you a building permit. The second document is the actual water hookup approval, which is granted once the property owner presents a fully stamped and certified building permit. This approval grants the user the right to purchase a water meter and to have unrestricted use of water.

Building in a foreign country is always a bit nerve-racking, but with the right information, there is a better chance things will go smoothly. Having honest and professional people on your side is critical, as is understanding the Costa Rican laws that affect your investment. Arming yourself with the above knowledge is the first step when house hunting in Costa Rica.

Building Your Home

My Husband: "We need more windows."
Me: "No. No, we do not."

There are some amazing homes in Costa Rica. Some with open courtyards revealing tropical gardens, and others with walls of glass built on mountaintops. The views are astounding, even in the most unremarkable places.

I remember walking through a mechanic's garage and finding a sweeping view of the Central Plateau in the rear of his building.

"Wow," I said.

"I love my country," the mechanic replied before he rolled himself underneath a car.

It's no wonder everyone's mind races when visiting, dreaming about whether they too can build a home here and start living the pura vida life. And you can if you do a little research and fully understand the practicalities of construction in a foreign country. Expect some surprises.

We've lived in a variety of houses around the country and found faulty electric, missing roof tiles, pipes that lead nowhere, and doors that open in the wrong direction. A common problem is improperly ventilated sewer pipes. That one is the worst! We knew when we built our home that we would have to find a competent builder, one who had many houses already under his belt. (You can read more about that hilarious year in *Happier Than A Billionaire: An Acre in Paradise.*)

If at all possible, it's best to be in Costa Rica so you can oversee the building process. I know a few people who built their homes while they were out of the country, only to return and find rooms that were too small or finishings that they never chose. These mishaps are not always due to a sinister contractor. Anytime you're dealing with different systems of measurements, unreliable utilities, and a language barrier, all from three thousand miles away, you can pretty much count on a hilariously tragic story or two. So please, supervise your construction so you don't return to find an Olympic-sized swimming pool and learn that you are now sixty million dollars over budget.

Building costs vary greatly depending on the style of finishes you choose and where you plan to build. Quotes range from $60 a square foot when building closer to San José, in places such as Grecia, to $80 to $150 per square foot if you're building near the beach. One reason things are more expensive at the beach is because of high fuel costs. The farther you are from San José, the more you'll pay for building materials.

Deciding whether to buy a house already built or to undergo the tedious process of constructing one will not be easy. However, purchasing an existing home will likely cost significantly more than building one yourself. It boils down to finances and how much energy you want to put into the project. If you decide to build, make sure you have the tenacity to see it through.

The Architect

The first step, and one that is required by law, is to hire an architect and engineer. I recommend you use one licensed by the Costa Rica Association of Engineers and Architects (Colegio Federado de Ingenieros y Arquitectos, also known as CFIA). Only a licensed architect can submit your plans to the municipality. The CFIA sets a minimum fee schedule, but there is no cap on how much one can charge.

One architect I recommend is José Pablo Acuna Lett, because he has been working with clients from the USA, Canada, the UK, France, Germany, and Russia for over ten years. He's also the architect that designed The Happier House! José was gracious and answered a few questions to help us better understand the process of designing a home in Costa Rica.

What is the first thing a foreigner should look for in an architect?

"When a foreigner is looking for an architect in Costa Rica, there are some important things to consider. Education is important. I studied at Tecnológico de Monterrey, a well-known university in Mexico, and I received my MBA specializing in international business. I travel a lot, and this exposes me to the many different building styles all around the world.

"If a person is not very confident with the Spanish language, communication will be easier with an English-speaking architect. It's a good idea to hire one who is knowledgeable about the area where you want to build and has experience. Always make sure your architect is a member of the CFIA."

What are the fees?

"The architectural, electrical, mechanical, structural, and A/C engineers charge a total of 10.5% of the projected building cost of the home," José explains. "This 10.5% is broken down into the following categories: 1.5% for preliminary studies and architectural design, 4% for architectural, electrical, plumbing, structural, A/C building plans and specifications, and 5% for site supervision by all professionals involved in the process during the time of construction."

What qualities make a good architect?

"I like to understand each client's needs and dreams. From the moment I meet a new client (in person or by email), I pay close attention to what they have in mind. Once I have a thorough understanding of their idea, I start the creative process. I always respond to a client's question or concern within twenty-four hours.

"I love all different types of architectural styles and have designed and built projects in Playas del Coco, Tamarindo, Playa Grande, Bay of Pirates, Conchal, Flamingo, Santa Teresa, and Punta Leona."

Where is your favorite place to build?

"Guanacaste has a special place in my heart. My parents brought me to Playas del Coco for the first time when I was four weeks old. It's always been my dream to be an architect in this area. I'm living my dream now, practicing my career in this paradise.

"Ecology and sustainable development are very important to me. I love working with alternative energy sources and bio-climatic architecture. I try to establish a good relationship with my clients beyond work to catch their essence and express it in the homes I design. Even though professional fees may not vary a lot from one architect to another (the CFIA sets a minimum fee schedule but there is no cap on how much one can charge), I always give my clients the very best deal I can. Living and working in the same area makes it easier for me because I don't have to charge for extra for travel expenses."

Are you familiar with the permit process in Guanacaste?

"I'm familiar with nearly every development in the area and have been personally involved with many. I have a strong understanding of Costa Rican bureaucracy, and this helps to move things along when applying for permits."

It's common for documents to get lost on someone's desk or be submitted to the wrong office. José makes sure that everything gets filed so that you don't find out five years down the line that you never officially had a building permit to begin with. A friend of mine is now facing this exact problem, and the amount of time it takes to rectify it is unbelievable.

The Builder

It's safe to say your Costa Rican home will be built using very strict earthquake codes. Our last major earthquake in Guanacaste was a doozy (7.6 on the Richter scale). It lasted for over a minute, and it felt like the house was exploding around us. It shook so much I couldn't even get our key into the metal gate at our front entrance. Finally, Rob pulled the keys out of my hands and was able to unlock it. Experts say not to run out of the house, since you're more likely to get killed by things falling on your head if you're outdoors. But our instincts told us to run... so we did. I'm surprised I didn't fall into a hole on the way out. I was a hysterical mess. I thought all my friends were dead, buried beneath a ton of rubble. Then there was the tsunami warning, which capped off the ultimate crappy days.

Before this episode, I always wondered if a big earthquake would expose inferior construction here like it often does in other countries around the world. Would we find newspaper stuffed into supporting columns, or a lack of rebar in concrete foundations? Thankfully, that didn't happen in Costa Rica. I feel much safer than I did before, and I'm confident that at the very least, most houses here have solid foundations.

I contacted our builder, Aaron, to hear his thoughts on construction.

What types of contracts are common with builders?

"A clear and solid contract with your builder is a great place to start," he says. "There are two common types of contracts: a line-item contract and a fixed-price contract. Let me explain the difference.

"In a line-item contact, the cost of labor is based on a percentage of the cost of your materials. The total cost of your project will be materials plus the agreed-upon percentage for labor. A fixed-price contract is exactly what it sounds like: the builder gives you one upfront price for the entire build.

"They both have advantages and disadvantages. One risk you take when choosing a line-item contract is that the cost of materials can fluctuate throughout the build, making it hard to predict the exact cost of the total project. The advantage of a fixed-price contract is that the client knows exactly what the home will cost. However, when creating a fixed-cost contract, builders will consider unforeseen circumstances. An estimated rising material cost will be factored into the quote, and all of this will usually lead to a higher price in the end."

Which do most prefer?

"Most of my clients prefer a line-item contract, as do I. If you have a good trusting relationship with your builder, this is usually the way to go. It's always a good idea to show up at the building site often in order to keep track of quality and the materials going into the project.

"Another important thing to consider is the climate in which you are building. A good design should have lots of cross ventilation and a good plan for outdoor living. Keeping radiant heat off a house is critical, and a lot of that can be accomplished with intelligent landscaping."

What are the most common building materials?

"There are three common ways most people choose to build in Costa Rica: concrete block, concrete/Styrofoam block, or steel stud. My clients can choose any of these, but I prefer steel because it goes up much faster and has an insulation rating of an R19. Concrete/Styrofoam block has an R19 insulation rating as well, but it's labor intensive and costs 20% more. Regular concrete block has a very poor insulation rating, so I'd rather not use it. Electricity is expensive in Costa Rica; it's critical that a house is well insulated in order to keep air conditioning costs down.

"I also favor steel because it's economical, better for the environment, creates less waste, and is not as cumbersome. It's easier to make adjustments or remodel later as well. For example, if you want to run a simple electrical line for another outlet, it's easy when using steel. If you have a house made of concrete block, it's much more time-consuming and expensive.

"I love my job and enjoy helping people build their dream homes. Having a good relationship with your builder is essential. I hate to say that I've seen some crazy stuff: retaining walls have been built out of roof tin, and drainage has been installed sending water back up against a house. Something very common in Costa Rica is plumbing being installed without proper ventilation. This will cause sewage gases to build up in the home, which smells terrible and can even become a health hazard. Always interview your builder, as well as his clients. A good builder will have no objection to letting you tour his projects."

Closing Costs

I reached out to a well-respected San José attorney, Alejandro Montealegre, for information regarding closing costs.

What terms will a contract have in regard to these costs?

"The law stipulates that, unless otherwise agreed by the parties, or legal disposition in contrary, the notary fees, registry fees, stamps and taxes, shall be paid by both parties (buyer and seller) in equal shares (50/50) except mortgages and their cancelations, which correspond 100% to the debtors.

"This means that, for example, ACME developer agrees to pay 50% of the notary fees of the mortgage, in case I'm appointed to be the notary authorizing the deed. If buyers are paying in cash for the property and decide to hire their own attorney-notary to draft the deed of transfer, buyers are responsible for paying 100% of the closing costs, except for my fees, which are paid separately by ACME. When part of the price of the purchase is financed by ACME, then ACME has the right to appoint me as the notary to draft the deed of transfer and the mortgage. In that case, ACME pays 50% of transfer fees, and buyers shall pay the remaining transfer fees, along with any fees for a mortgage, all transfer taxes, registry fees, and stamps of the deed."

Luxury Tax: This tax is to be paid by people who own residential properties in Costa Rica with a total value of approximately $229,600.00 USD or higher. The value of a property is determined by taking into account the value of the main construction plus the value of all permanent installations (pool, patio, etc.). If this value exceeds the amount mentioned above, then the cost of the land must be calculated and added to the value. This tax starts at a minimum of .25% for properties of up to $574,940.00 USD and in increments of 0.05%, with a max of 0.55% for properties whose value exceeds an approximate $3,458,540.00 USD.

Links:

Aaron the Builder: acberkowitzmv@gmail.com

Ale Elliot, Mar Vista Project Manager:
www.marvistacr.com

Architect: José Pablo Acuna Lett, MBA
JPA Architecture and Planning
Email: jpalett@gmail.com
Tele: 2271-1965 Cell: 8830-4827

Costa Rica Association of Engineers and Architects:
www.cfia.or.cr

Halloween Crab
Variegated
Squirrel

Blathering

Rob Wants a Weedwacker

"A few fly bites cannot stop a spirited horse." ~ Mark Twain

One reason I named my last book *Happier Than A Billionaire: An Acre in Paradise* is because Rob has cultivated, tended to, and nurtured our land into a fairy-tale environment. There is not one inch of this property that hasn't been touched by my adorable Italian gardener.

However, it quickly became clear he needed more than his machete to manage the property, so he began searching for a weedwacker. A good one that cost $250 in the United States cost $800 in Costa Rica. He was faced with quite the conundrum. So against his better judgment, he bought the cheapest one in our local store.

I loved this power tool. The squirrely hum of the motor made me smile. It was cute, featherlight, and designed for manicuring a four-by-four-square-foot piece of grass in front of your condominium... in your bathrobe... on Sunday morning.

I could tell Rob was skeptical; he is not a weedwacker hobbyist but a professional who spends a majority of his day whacking away in his high rubber boots, plastic glasses, and a hat with flaps covering his neck and ears. He looks creepy, like that questionable person you would never follow into an elevator. I'll take my chances in the darkened stairwell, thank you.

I left him to his work and returned ten minutes later to find no whacking of weeds. The head had already stopped spinning—the weedwacker's, that is, not my husband's. His turned a shade of raspberry jam.

Rob promptly took it to a local mechanic, who fixed it for $30. And it took thirty minutes before it broke down completely. It was a commendable death, with the squirrely spin of the motor sputtering until the last squirrel called it quits.

"Just bite the bullet and buy the more expensive one," I suggested.

"No bullets will be bit. I'll ask Mr. Dinkleman to haul one down from the States."

The Dinklemans were the first couple to stay at The Happier House. They enjoyed their accommodations so much they were returning in a few months.

"You can't ask the Dinklemans to lug a weedwacker onto a plane. I only ask for printer ink from people. And that fits in a shoe."

But Rob couldn't hear me over the phone conversation he was having with a weedwacker store in the United States. A three-pronged approach was hatched. With spirited enthusiasm, Mr. Dinkleman would:

1. Retrieve the weedwacker from the store.
2. Carefully repack it to avoid damage.
3. Carry it to the airport. You know, because people love to haul weedwackers with them on vacation.

Remarkably, Mr. Dinkleman said yes.

When Rob ordered it over the phone, the salesman offered to test it out first.

"Please," my husband pleaded, "don't, for any reason, fill it with gas. It has to go onto an airplane."

"But there's no warranty unless I test it."

"Do you have a warranty shop in Costa Rica?"

"No."

"Exactly. Skip it."

Mr. Dinkleman cheerfully went along with this delicious plan and picked up the weedwacker, packed it in two long boxes filled with Styrofoam peanuts, and taped the boxes together.

"Ah, this will go swimmingly," I imagined him saying. But once at the airport, they ran into an issue. It was a formidable obstacle that anyone who travels has encountered: the lady at the ticket counter.

"Sir, please declare what is in that box," she demanded.

"I declare it is a weedwacker," he said, smiling and bubbling with fervor.

"Is it gas or electric?" With the tiny scent of petroleum and failure in the air, decisions had to be made. And they had to be made quickly.

"It is gas. I declare it is gas," he announced.

It turns out the conscientious salesman had ultimately tested the weedwacker before selling it. Good news was it had a warranty. Bad news was that it was not allowed on the plane because airlines frown upon nail clippers and carry-ons smelling of gasoline.

The couple was already late for their flight, so Mr. Dinkleman told his wife, "If I don't return in time, go on without me." It was a noble gesture that she took him up on by disappearing down the terminal.

He sprinted back to his car, opened his hatchback, and hastily shoved the weedwacker inside. Subsequently, the box popped and exploded one million Styrofoam peanuts into his car, the surrounding parking lot, and all over Mr. Dinkleman. May I remind you, I only ask guests to haul printer ink.

Fortunately, Mr. Dinkleman caught his flight and enjoyed another holiday at The Happier House. He even felt bad about the situation. That's how nice this guy is. Since this left us in the same position we were in before, I told Rob to just suck it up and buy the $800 weedwacker from the hardware store.

"Absolutely not. Mr. Dinkleman said he'll ship it once he returns to the United States." And he did mail the weedwacker to Miami, where we hired a mail service to ship it to Costa Rica.

"They'll even deliver it to our development!" Rob exclaimed. If you don't know anything about reliable Costa Rican mail delivery, I'll fill you in: there is none. Not rain, or snow, or even a perfect sunny day will get your package to arrive anywhere on time.

So we waited for months while Rob toiled away in the garden with his machete. Finally, we received an email stating our weedwacker had been delivered to a bus station over an hour away. The shipping company placed it on a bus seat with the pointed head staring longingly out the window as it traveled throughout the Costa Rican countryside.

When it was all said and done, that weedwacker—the one we shipped because my husband refused to pay $800 for it here in Costa Rica—cost us $850.

"You know, you could have just bought it here... right down the road," I hinted. "We wouldn't have had to involve our guests, or find a shipping company, or travel an hour to pick it up."

"I actually feel pretty good about the whole thing," he said. He eagerly filled it with gas before disappearing into the weeds.

Entertaining the Guests

When my guests arrive at The Happier House, I want them to imagine it's a vacation home that has been in their family for years. A place that feels familiar; a small corner of the world to decompress from their stressful lives. It's important they have the best experience, so I take on the responsibility of Jeeves—or some New Jersey version of it—by providing them with the necessities one might find in the home of an author who makes her living writing about the stupid things her husband does.

I provide seashell-embroidered towels that my mother hauled in her luggage. There was a steep discount at Kohl's, so she Mad Maxed her way down the crowded aisle, pushed other customers out of the way, and used her cane to knock fifty towels off the shelves and into her cart. People questioned her urgency, but she barely said a word. One does not converse with the competition during a White Sale.

Taking ideas from five-star reviews of fancy resorts, I add special touches to each room. Bathroom soap dispensers smell of jasmine, and sheets are a thread count of high number, not at all like the linens I slept on as a kid. The Sears 40-grit road rash line took 1976 by storm. It had a proprietary blend of attic insulation and thumbtacks, contributing to my childhood insomnia and causing me to sneak out of my room at 10 p.m. to watch *Charlie's Angels*. But I loved shopping at Sears, a glorious store where a kid could simultaneously fondle a Black & Decker chainsaw while browsing for a Scooby-Doo Mystery Machine.

Toys were thoughtfully positioned just an aisle away from the tool department; the precise distance a kid could sneak away unnoticed to climb on top a 16-horsepower John Deere riding tractor with a low-tone muffler system. You're never too young to experience the adrenaline high of felicitous lawn maintenance.

While I tend to the domestication of running our Happier empire, Rob disappears into the garden for variable lengths of time. Some so long it's probable that a colossal ant mound swallowed him whole. So every thirty minutes, I walk out onto the balcony to listen for the distant hum of his weedwacker. It's my Lojack system and my assurance that he's still alive.

It's unnerving when Rob works in the garden because he's easily distracted. His mind is an amusement park, but not Six Flags or Hershey Park. More like the ones you'd see on a boardwalk— rides with questionable safety standards, fun house mirrors, and games of chance along the periphery. He's always thinking about what's for dinner, which usually causes him to drift off dreaming of his mother's delicious chicken cutlets, before bouncing back to memories of driving a gypsy cab. These distractions often result in accidentally machete-ing a hibiscus plant that's home to a nest of surly wasps. My husband never once calculates the odds of surviving sixty-five angry stings. I do, thus the thirty-minute Rob safety check.

Today, I take note of his weedwacker hum before heading inside to enjoy passing the hours reading a book. Nothing makes a bibliophile happier than solitude paired with a page-turner. And it was. I couldn't put it down until the story lulled me into an afternoon nap. It was, by all accounts, the perfect day.

Later that afternoon, I walk downstairs to assist my guests by drawing maps to beaches with squishy marshmallow sand, only to find them concerned over an incident they just witnessed while sunning themselves beside the pool.

"How's your husband doing?" one of my guest inquires in a tone that would have me suspect Rob was, at one time, doing something worth inquiring about. It's not uncommon for people to ask about him, since he's the fun one in our relationship and tells humorous anecdotes about his car catching fire while crossing the Verrazzano-Narrows Bridge. They win the crowd over every time. I reminisce about wearing braces for four years. Crowds disperse.

"We didn't know what to do, so we watched from a distance," my guest continues before lowering his voice. He leans in closer, displaying an expression of concern. "Just in case he fell in further."

Well, this is news to me. I do recall a pause in the weedwacking, because as I previously mentioned, I reclined mid-afternoon for a sojourn from my Rob Death Watch shift.

After inquiring about the fate of my husband, I discover that, due to his daydreaming about lasagna, he inadvertently fell through the flimsy plastic lid covering our underground water tank.

"We saw him through the palm trees," my guest explains, "but we didn't want to embarrass him and didn't know whether to help or just observe. We chose to observe."

And what my guests observed was Rob's one leg stuck inside the tank, with the other spread-eagled across our lawn. I would suggest to anyone who finds themselves in a similar predicament that this is the precise time to call for assistance. A subdued "Excuse me, sir, would you mind lending me a hand?" would suffice. But Rob prides himself on never... ever... asking anyone for help.

Unfortunately, this isn't Rob's first rodeo in absurdity. He once tried to retrieve his scooter from a mechanic who already closed his doors for the night. My husband decided to sneak inside the pitch-dark garage, only to find a few very surprised Rottweilers, and on his attempt to leave, he plummeted into a bay pit. He returned home with a pizza and a bashed shin. He ate the pizza first before tending to the shin. At least what happened just now occurred on our property without any risk of being mauled to death. Today was simply another visit to his amusement park, but without a pizza.

I glance through the palm trees, the same vantage point as my guests, but don't see my husband.

"Did he fall all the way through?" I ask, surely expecting to find my husband treading water.

"No. We wouldn't have allowed that. After a bit of a struggle, he pulled himself out. Is there a place to rent kayaks?"

Yes, there is a place to rent kayaks. Maps are drawn, and soon I hear the comforting sound of Rob's weedwacker. I finish with my guests and thank them for caring about the fate of my husband. They appear unfazed and leave the house with the expression of someone who had just suffered through a Best of Broadway production aboard a Carnival Cruise Line.

I follow the weedwacker hum and find him at a forty-five-degree angle, whacking weeds with his typical exuberance.

"You're good?" I yell.

"Yeah. What's for dinner?" he replies before stepping into an ant mound.

Rob doesn't mention anything about the water tank until a week later, when we stop by a hardware store. He pulls the broken tank lid from the backseat.

"I had a situation" is all he says before entering the store and purchasing another flimsy lid that cost a not-so-flimsy sixty dollars.

This incident was a highlight for my guests, which makes me consider adding Rob to the amenities. It wouldn't hurt for him to learn a medley of "Some Enchanted Evening," "All that Jazz," and "If I Were a Rich Man" to charm the crowd before needing rescue. I'll list him as entertainment, and place it between the seashell-embroidered towels and free Wi-Fi.

As for the water tank, it's only a matter of time before he falls through it again. I could arrange orange cones around the perimeter. Maybe even an actual construction worker waving red flags, directing Rob toward safer territory.

Until then, I'll listen for that weedwacker hum and be grateful that there isn't a Sears nearby that sells John Deere tractors. A ride I don't want to see at Rob's amusement park.

Don't Share This Book

Reviews are a funny thing. People enjoy reading them because it helps provide insight into the quality of a product. When someone dislikes your product, and possibly your personality, they hasten to their desktop.

Why their desktop? Because I can't believe an angry person has the patience to type these reviews on a smartphone. No one has the dexterity for that. I can hardly add the right emoji when I text my sister. She sent me the "100" emoji with two red lines underneath. I had no idea what that meant until today. "Keep it 100%," my niece told me. Keep what 100%? The fact that my husband fell into our water tank? Seventy-eight percent is more my speed. Eighty-two percent on a good day.

My last *Escape Manual* was published two years ago and has accumulated many good reviews. Except it's been brought to my attention that my copyright page includes an odd sentence: "This book may not be resold or given away to other people."

I'm not sure why it's there, but since this book has business links and stories of individuals, I had to insert a disclaimer. I probably found legal jargon on the internet, and this line must have been included. I never even noticed.

A gentleman took considerable offense to this passage. He bought my book, only to learn it stymied his prolific book-sharing enterprise. I leaned back and imagined his anger. This guy was clearly upset by my copyright page, a page that I have never bothered to read in any book I have ever owned. I don't even read the terms of service when I download an app or update my Microsoft operating system. For all I know, I've accepted offers to work the engine room on a Russian submarine.

I can't blame his discontent with my Orwellian proclamation, and I wholeheartedly apologize to all who were outraged. Everyone should share my book and not be concerned I'll interrogate them. I encourage you to resell it to Martha on bingo night or lend it to Henry in accounting. Hell, stick it in the garage, since that's where my dad says all travel books end up anyway.

But this reviewer couldn't bottle his outrage any longer. He went posthaste to his desktop to give me a spectacular schooling of the Supreme Court's decision on "first sale doctrine." There's no way he could have done this on his iPhone. Have you ever angrily typed on a small device? There's no satisfaction in it. But a desktop keyboard? That sounds like the *Washington Post* newsroom during Watergate.

"Sorry to be the one to break it to you," he types, "but you can't do that with books as it is against the law!"

Holy cow, I'm in trouble. He's already bringing the feds into this.

"And for that, I shall ding you another star, and I won't even give you a nice try!" I shall take that ding, Amazon reviewer. The buck stops with the Happier lady. But not even a nice try? That just seems mean.

"Anyone can resell your book or even make other 'fair uses' of it per US laws, so no, you can't say that in your book as it is bologna."

Bologna? He must eat his on toast points. I have a more blue-collar relationship with this delicacy and pronounce it baloney, the way God intended. And I happen to love it! My mom prepared this culinary delight for me every day, slapped between two pieces of Wonder Bread and slathered in mayonnaise. I've calculated that I've eaten over five thousand of these nitrate sandwiches before the age of twelve, which some have alluded to be the reason for my gnome-like stature. Now if you compared my book to olive loaf, the fruitcake of deli meat, that would have hurt.

Unfortunately, the bologna didn't stop there. This reviewer put a comment below his own review. "And another thing," he begins. Oh, brother. That's never a good sign.

Have you ever met anyone who started a conversation with "and another thing" that isn't argumentative? "We rode Space Mountain and then took pictures at Cinderella's Castle. And another thing... it was awesome." That doesn't ring true, right? "Your brother's a drunk and ruined Thanksgiving. And another thing... he owes me money," sounds a lot more genuine.

In a lengthy dissertation, the reviewer cited how much he did not appreciate my blathering. Good call, Chief Justice. Boy, can I be annoying. Just ask my husband: he'll agree with you, and that guy loves me. This chap must not have read my other books, which are stuffed with enough blather to fill the Library of Congress. Ironically, a place where I can learn more about this "first sale doctrine." On a literary note, I do appreciate the more pretentious use of "blather" instead of "blabber." I would have chosen the latter, but then again, I went to public school and dined on artisanal Wonder Bread.

My pal continued his pep talk and went for the proverbial nail in the coffin. "Speaking tirelessly about your 'idiot and incompetent' husband isn't that funny and does not make you sound smart either."

This is my kind of reviewer, and I'd love to meet him at Applebee's. I never sound smart, so now the pressure is off. The bar is set low, which is precisely the location where I need the bar to be when meeting new people.

But after all that, the guy gave me a pleasant three stars, and it was a pleasant way to end this dynamic between both of us. I wanted to know more about him, so I perused his other reviews, where I find he gave hot sauce a whopping five stars. "It is truly the right amount of heat." I have a competitive streak, so I construct a plan to win him back: my next *Escape Manual* must pair nicely with steak.

This critic got me thinking. Telling someone not to share my book is pretty badass of me. I've never been labeled a tough gal, so I wonder if this guy thought there would be repercussions for this offense. He's missing the biggest part of my master plan. If someone tipped me off to him lending my book out, he's got bigger problems. There's a rat in his house.

I imagine showing up in a trench coat on his front porch. His wife, expecting a hot sauce shipment, will open the door only to find me standing there.

"We don't want any trouble," she'll say. She'll attempt to slam the door, but I'll insert my foot before it closes.

"I'm not interested in you. It's your husband I'm looking for."

As I follow her to the kitchen, I'll notice the bookshelves in the living room. The *Escape Manual* is not there. It's confirmed; my book has been shared.

The reviewer sits down, nervous, with the first sale doctrine in hand. He clumsily flips through while asking for a glass of water. He's parched. All that hot sauce heat is getting to him.

I explain that I'm not here to arrest, only to deliver a citation. And that citation includes hours of me blathering about my idiot and incompetent husband. I cover the Billboard top hits, like the gun in the fireplace story, and continue on to him falling off his scooter while delivering my impressive stool sample to a doctor.

By the time I'm finished, it's dawn. The wife peeks out the bedroom door before slamming it shut. I think we've learned who the rat was.

I put on my fedora and tell Chief Justice that I'll see myself out. I'm off to confront Billy Ray in Biloxi, Mississippi. He lent my book to Parker at the Kiwanis spaghetti dinner fundraiser.

But before I do, I keep it 100% by making myself a baloney sandwich. I use all his mayonnaise and cut the crust off the Wonder Bread. It's a long bus ride to Biloxi. My blathering crusade carries on.

Email From Dad

From: Nadine
Sent: 1:44 PM
To: Dad
Subject: He Really Gives It to Me

Hi Dad,

Boy, did I just get hammered on the *Escape Manual.* I mistakenly included this weird sentence on the copyright page that really ticked off a reviewer. And he even came back to put a comment on his own review.

I'm not sure why that sentence is even on the page, I must have copied and pasted it without noticing. Big mistake on my part.

Nadine

From: Dad
Sent: 3:10 AM
To: Nadine
Subject: RE: He Really Gives It to Me

Nadine,

I have read many reviews, good, bad and in between. But this review (and the review of his own review) is something different. This one actually scares me. After reading this, I finally understand what Hannah Arendt meant by the "banality of evil."

Now I am not saying this reviewer is evil, but I am saying he has a lobotomized, fossilized, bureaucratic mindset, where his inflexible set of rules takes precedence over common sense and normal human behavior. His review tells me more about him than it does about the author or the *Escape Manual.* It tells me he lives a robotic life of bitterness, anger, malice, and frustration. And the scary part is this: he thinks he is behaving in a rational manner.

Now it's my understanding that, when an author publishes a book they stick in those semi-contractual things and copyright phraseology as a matter of course. Does anyone actually look for these just to have an "I gotcha" moment? It's a perfunctory thing. It's like the small print when you're applying for a car loan. Who the hell reads it or cares?

But this guy... he chose to give his undivided attention and regale us with his wisdom. His actions and motivations remind me of the missing strawberries in *The Caine Mutiny,* with Captain Queeg triumphantly telling all how he solved this mystery.

Shakespeare said, "The play's the thing," and in this case I would like to remind this jerk, the book's the thing along with all of the helpful information therein.

But even more than this, in his out-of-control self-importance, this guy wrote a review of his own review. And it included marriage counseling. I have a message for this plodding, lugubrious nonentity... lighten up.

This is not an emergency, and I have matured above my conduct with previous computer problems that you have solved for me. On Mom's computer, the damn AOL gold icon disappeared. I hit the little arrow point on the bottom right-hand side of the computer, but the icon still did not appear. Discuss this with your sister to collaborate an appropriate course of action.

Daddy

Excalibur

I'm back in New Jersey watching my niece perform in a Catholic elementary school production of *Grease.* Unlike the original version containing saucy adult themes, this is a sanitized adaptation, where the craziest thing Sandy does is get her ears pierced. As per the original script, Sandy is transformed at the end of the show, wearing a leather jacket but makes it clear to Danny that he'll only be holding her hand. Good for her. My Scottish grandfather would have applauded her Puritan values. After the high of seeing my niece hand-jive in the last row of the chorus, the very last thing I want to do during my visit is to pack a food dehydrator. Rob is growing an enormous amount of fruit, so to deal with the inventory, he ordered the largest one he could find and shipped it to my parents' house.

"It's made in the USA!" he cheers over the phone. I like these surprises, almost as much as my father asking me to partake in our family's Squirrel Attic Deportation festival. This year's theme: "Why is your stuff still in our attic? The squirrels are whizzing all over it."

Rob has a vision for our property, and that vision includes scores of trees, which are now producing scores of fruits. My favorites are the watermelon and squash patches, both of which grow in our driveway. I like to call them driveway fruit and plan to pitch them on the Home Shopping Network.

"See here, Karen?" I'll say while pointing to sliced watermelon. "These beauties grew right next to our pile of broken roof tiles, and can be yours with only three Easy Pays."

I'm fascinated by QVC and the Home Shopping Network. When I'm not on a Rob Death Watch, I love surfing their websites, qvc- and hsn.com. Look how easy that is to type. They shortened their names down to three letters. I should have thought of that before calling my website happierthanabillionaire.com. And you know what's worse? My email: puravida@happierthanabillionaire.com. I can hardly spell that, and I'm the schmuck who came up with it.

After logging on, I look for the dumbest product on their schedule. Then I check to see which jamoke is selling it. I spend an inordinate amount of time wondering about the lives of these segment hosts.

I imagine they drag themselves into the break room each morning and pour a tepid four-hour-old cup of coffee from a busted Cuisinart, one that had been returned due to a faulty programmable clock. They used to have the Keurig Elite, but upper management would only provide refillable pods. Coffee grounds spilled everywhere. Brian, the leader in shower radio sales, gave a rousing *Norma Mae* speech on the break table before marching into the warehouse and stealing the broken Cuisinart. Morale is low.

Over muddy coffee, they peruse their schedule and learn what products each of them will be pitching that day. Karen finds out she's responsible for twenty minutes of enthusiastic air time hocking a set of four Garfield porcelain figurines.

Who can talk about Garfield figurines for twenty minutes? I can tell you who. Me, but that's only because I can't shut up. Karen gets this lousy gig because she hasn't yet achieved Gold Tier status. Those hosts get the juicy merchandise, like Liza Minnelli's sequined apparel line. And they have a different break room, with a cappuccino machine and massaging recliner.

Right now I'm watching Greg peddle jumbo Dutch holiday tulips. He sells the bulbs with a decorative container and explains that if I reside in an assisted living home, this could replace my Christmas tree. What a peculiar thing to say.

He explains that these flowers last two weeks, and diligently demonstrates how to water them, which remarkably involves a glass of... wait for it ... water. I have to admit, Greg, I'm glad you're taking me through all the steps. This is something I would excel at while living in a Boca Raton nursing facility. And I could surely use the entertainment in between my rigorous hallway walking and afternoon ceiling gazing.

I remind myself that I already have a massive garden and tend to none of it. I'm more of a garden admirer who does all the admiring while my husband does all the gardening. So far that's worked in our relationship and shall continue henceforth. But I love the idea of putting my hands in soil, as long as the soil is directly in front of me, on the coffee table, in a climate-controlled room.

But let's get back to the problem at hand. Because we have so many papayas, watermelons, bananas, and plantains growing, Rob ordered the biggest dehydrator he could find: the behemoth Excalibur model. As Karen would pitch, "It has nine trays totaling fifteen square feet of drying space for your favorite snacks! No tray rotation required. Who has time for that?"

And you're right, Karen. I don't have time for that. Thank you, Rob, for considering me for this job. I was just telling my sister how much I yearned to fly the friendly skies with a food dehydrator the size of a dog kennel. I imagine it busting through my luggage like the two 25 lb. barbell plates Rob packed years ago. What came out along the baggage carousel was our suitcase split in half and two plates lagging behind on the conveyor belt. "What kind of idiot packs gym plates?" a guy said behind me at the precise moment Rob reached for the bag.

I come up with a dozen excuses not to pack it, until I remember the story of King Arthur. "Who so pulleth out this Excalibur sword from this stone must be loyal and pure of heart. He shall be king born of England!" These rotating trays were delivered into my hands for safe passage to Costa Rica. As stupid as it sounds, this is my quest, and I shall be king of tasty snacks if I succeed.

I first consider keeping it in the box and tying a rope around it. That's what Mr. Dinkleman did when he brought our weedwacker to the airport. This sounds easy enough, until I realize I can't manage the box. It's just too big.

I then decide to buy an oversized duffel bag. I cram it inside, but there's no room for any padding around the corners. It barely zips shut and looks like a snake that ate a giant Rubik's Cube. As I ponder this predicament, my mother yells over my shoulder. She has a patented formula for packing, but her trips never involve lugging car parts, gym equipment, or food dehydrators overseas.

"You can't carry that to the airport! It's too big," she screams. She's a retired schoolteacher who still reprimands me for not knowing all fifty state capitals. "Don't be stupid," she'll scold after I say Chicago is the capital of Illinois. My mom would make a horrible HSN host. Every person calling in would get admonished, which in retrospect would make a better show than watching Greg water tulip bulbs.

"They'll take it as long as I don't fill it with gasoline. And shouldn't you be helping Dad get squirrels out of the attic?" She obviously doesn't understand I'm loyal and pure of heart. It's my mission to get this into my husband's fertilizing hands.

I hand-jive my way to the airport, make my way to the counter, and drop the duffel bag onto the scale. The lady curiously looks down before saying, "Ma'am, please declare what's in that box."

"I declareth the Excalibur nine-tray food dehydrator."

"Did you pack that bag yourself?"

"Unfortunately, it takes my own personal level of stupidity to pull this off."

Before the woman can ask more questions, she becomes distracted over the couple arguing next to me. They're attempting to remove ten pounds of stuff out of an overweight suitcase. Maybe they're carrying porcelain figurines. That would be just as dumb as packing this food dehydrator. Without hesitation, the airline attendant takes my luggage and sends me on my way. When I land in Costa Rica, I find my giant Rubik's Cube on the carousel, in good condition except for one damaged corner. It's a small price to pay.

Once I'm home, Rob cuts up thirty pounds of fruit and makes delicious treats with the consistency of taffy. After a few bites, I spit out the consistency of my molar filling. Seventy dollars later, my dentist instructs me not to eat any more of it, which is a shame, because my freezer is now jam-packed with tooth-damaging snacks.

Legend has it that one must return Excalibur by tossing it back into an enchanted lake. I'm not doing that after the hassle of bringing it down. Instead, it'll sit on our counter until the next round of nine—no need to rotate—trays of fruit are ready to go. My reward is watching how happy it makes the most loyal and pure-hearted person in my life.

*This is ridiculous. I went on for hours and taught you nothing about Costa Rica. Now aren't you happy I created a blathering section in my book?

Road Trips

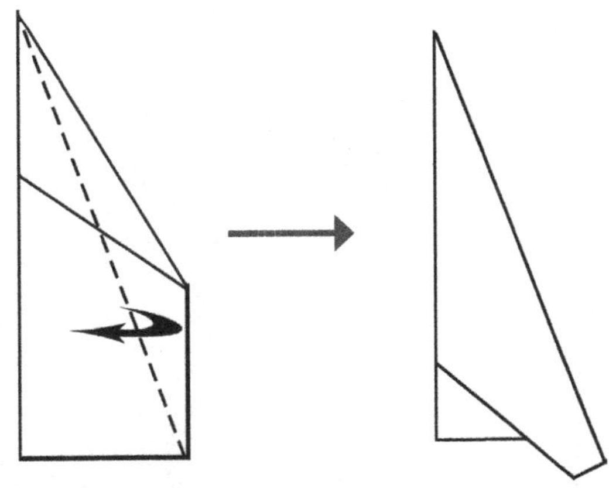

Fold at crease

The Famous Grecia Church

The Central Valley

"All good things are wild and free."
~ Henry David Thoreau

Many of you will be starting your adventure right here. You flew into the San José Airport, rented a car, and are ready to experience that magical Pura Vida everyone is talking about. The Central Valley includes the provinces of Alajuela, Heredia, San José, and Cartago. If you're a volcano lover, this is the place to be: Poás, Barva, Turrialba, and Irazú volcanoes are just a drive away.

It's cold on top of volcanoes, so be prepared! It's the only place in all of Costa Rica where I'm in pictures wearing a winter jacket.

San José The capital of Costa Rica is about 20 minutes from the airport depending on traffic, and I'm thrilled to announce that they finally installed street signs. Does that make it any easier to navigate? The answer is no. I find it nearly as confusing, since blocks often turn into one-way streets. Also, everyone still gives you weird landmarks that don't exist. My lawyer once told me to turn right at a mango tree. But that mango tree wasn't there anymore. And what kind of landmark is that? Why didn't he say "turn right at the flip-flop," since that's just as confusing as an invisible tree?

The following are three popular hotels near the airport:

Marriott: www.marriott.com/hotels/hotel-photos/sjocr-costa-rica-marriott-hotel-san-José

Intercontinental: www.ihg.com/hotels/us/en/reservation

Best Western Costa Rica: www.bestwesterncostarica.com

Top Three Attractions Worth Visiting

The Gold Museum (Museos del Banco Central) Adults $11, Students $8, under 12 free | Monday through Sunday, 9:15 a.m. to 5:00 p.m. | Address: Located in a subterranean building underneath the Plaza de la Cultura | This museum has a wonderful collection of gold items that date from 500 B.B. to 1500 A.D. For those interested in coins, the National Coin Museum is located in the same building.

The National Theatre of Costa Rica 9:00 a.m. to 5:00 p.m. | Tel: 2010-1100 | Address: Second Avenue and Fifth Street | Home to the National Symphony Orchestra, this beautiful building is worthy of a tour. Beautifully decorated, *USA Today* declared it as having one of the most admirable ceilings in the world.

The National Museum of Costa Rica Adults $9, Students $4 | Tuesday to Saturday, 8:30 a.m. to 4:30 p.m., Sunday 9:00 a.m. to 4:30 p.m. | Address: Street 17, between Central and Second Avenue | From relics of the Spanish invasion to pre-Columbian artifacts, this museum will entertain anyone who enjoys learning about the history and culture of a country. There's also a lovely butterfly garden in the courtyard!

You will probably notice stone spheres in front of museums, and throughout your travels. Some can be as small as a few inches in diameter while others are as large as six feet. At first glance, I thought they were lawn ornaments. But this is not your typical gnome or plastic flamingo. These have major historical significance.

It's believed these spheres trace back to the Isthmo-Colombian area and were carved from stone between 200 B.C. and 1500 A.D. They were initially found by workers clearing land for banana plantations. And what did the workers do upon their discovery? They blew them up, thinking there was gold inside!

No one is quite sure why these spheres were sculpted. It could have been to worship war gods or as a symbol of power.

Either way, they're amazing. Costa Rica may not have a Valley of the Kings, but its archeological presence is growing. Take that, Egypt. Costa Rica has balls!

Cartago Cartago is considered one of the oldest towns in the country and was the capital until 1832. It sits at the base of the Irazú Volcano, Costa Rica's largest and most active volcano. On calm days, you can drive or hike to the top and discover its beautiful blue lake nestled inside the Diego de la Haya crater. On a clear day, you can see both the Caribbean Sea and the Pacific Ocean. The park closes at 3:30 p.m.

Much of Cartago was destroyed in 1732 by an eruption of Irazú Volcano. In the city's central plaza, you'll find the Santiago Apóstol Parish Ruins. It is not a true "ruin," but an unfinished building damaged in the 1910 earthquake. It's worth a visit for picture taking and for strolling around the lovely gardens.

While in Cartago, stop by the huge white cathedral, where a pilgrimage occurs every year on August 2, at the Basílica de Nuestra Señora de Los Ángeles. According to legend, a girl found a statue of the black virgin (La Negrita) in 1635 and took it home. The next day, it miraculously appeared on the same rock where it was found. This rock is now located inside the cathedral, and hundreds of thousands of people come here every year to pray for miracles.

Turrialba If you see a volcano erupting on the news, most likely it's Turrialba. At times, the San José Airport closes down due to the ash. The park is closed indefinitely.

The Ruins of Guayabo de Turrialba $6 | 8:
3:30 p.m. daily | If you're interested in archeology, C
a must-see: an archeological site at the base of the Turrialba volcano. It dates between 1000 B.C. and 1400 A.D., and it's one of the most memorable places I've visited in Costa Rica.

The site, surrounded by a dense forest, contains ancient bridges, foundations of homes, tombs, and petroglyphs that date back three thousand years. A sophisticated aqueduct system carried water throughout the city, which was estimated to have 10,000 inhabitants at one time. But my favorite artifacts are the stone roads that lead into the forest. These roads are so well crafted, one might think they were gazing at the Roman Forum. We often believe civilization started with the Roman Empire, while in reality, other cultures were developing their cities long before Rome ever existed.

It's truly a mystical experience to stand in the center of these ruins and look up at the Turrialba Volcano. Since it's not yet a huge tourist attraction (half of it hasn't even been excavated), you will have plenty of quiet moments to reflect on what life was like in this newly unburied town.

Sarchi This town is the home of one of the biggest oxcart manufacturers in Costa Rica. It's fun to stop by the town center and view the huge, colorful ones on display. Oxcarts used to be the only means of transporting coffee beans across the country. Like having a well-engineered car today, it was important to have a well-crafted oxcart. Painting them served an important purpose. Each region had its own design, so one could identity where the driver was coming from by the pattern on his wheels. It gives one a nostalgic feeling to see Ticos still using these carts today to transport things short distances.

Sarchi is also home to many artists. One can find an assortment of beautiful souvenirs here. Even though we lived in a furnished home, we couldn't resist buying rocking chairs made in Sarchi, each one unique, with their seats made from strips of embossed leather. Chances are you've seen these chairs for sale at the airport.

Grecia If you've read my first book, you already know I started this grand adventure in Grecia. The reason Rob and I started there was because of the unremarkable decision to buy a car. It's probably the most unglamorous reason to move anywhere.

Grecia is well known for its many car lots. We thought we would stay in Grecia for six months and move on to the beach. But we fell in love with the town and realized there is so much to do in this part of the country. Not to mention we needed to get our driver's licenses and start the residency process.

I love this town. If I write any more about it, I fear someone will think I work for the Grecia Chamber of Commerce. But indulge me a bit more so I can share a few more facts and explain why it's such a great place.

The town of Grecia is unique in that it lies at the foot of a number of mountain ridges. I remember driving through and looking up at all those hills. I'd never considered living in the mountains before, but once in Grecia, I couldn't imagine living without these amazing views. There are days the clouds are so close, you can reach out and touch them.

Each ridge has a different feel, but they all have one thing in common: the higher you go, the cooler it gets. It's not rare to experience a drop in temperature of ten degrees within a fifteen-minute drive. If you would like to avoid buying a car, the bus service here is excellent on any of these ridges. Or you may choose to live in town so that you can easily walk to the market and local amenities.

Hotel Mango Valley Tel: 244-8833 www.mangovalley.com | Views, views, and more views. Cute, clean cottages with a friendly staff.

Iglesia de la Nuestra Señora de las Mercedes

The biggest, most venerable structure in all of Grecia is the red, metal church in the town's square. It was imported from Belgium in the 1890s and beautifully manicured gardens surround the perimeter. Across the street is an ice cream shop. Grab a cone, sit on one of the park benches, and watch the children as they dart around its fountain.

It's fun to watch how people interact here, and it doesn't take long to notice that Costa Ricans move at a different pace. People walk slower, stop to talk to one another and smile at you as they walk past. You'll instantly begin to feel a connection with the community. I think it's one of the things we tend to lose in a fast-paced society. We forget to stop and smile. Grecia reminded me how much I missed that.

Rob and I used to drive up and down many of Grecia's mountain ranges on our scooter. One of our favorite spots was San Luis de Grecia. It is a lovely town, and the views get more spectacular the higher you go. There are a couple places to stop for coffee at the top.

If you're in the mood for a walk and some bird-watching, you can find Bosque del Niño park at the top of the San Isidro de Grecia ridge. This is where the kinkajou I wrote about in my first book jumped onto our windowsill and scared the bejeezus out of us. You'll find this park full of wildlife, and it's a wonderful place to hike or have a picnic.

On the weekends, don't forget to check out the farmers' market across from the Judicial Building. The market is open on Friday after 3 p.m., and all day Saturday. The prices are great, and it was a big reason we could live on such a tight budget while in Grecia. We bought most of our food there. I would frequent the same vendors, and they were always nice to us. It's also a great place to work on your Spanish. It's a shame my husband told everybody there he was going to punch them instead of pay them (I taught him the wrong word for "pay," which is remarkably similar to "punch"). This may be the reason everyone was so nice to us.

Just like at the park, the pace at the market is slow. People stop dead center in a crowded aisle to say hello to a neighbor or a friend. They'll kiss each other on the cheek and hold up pedestrian traffic behind them. Nobody huffs or puffs. It's a wonderful way to live.

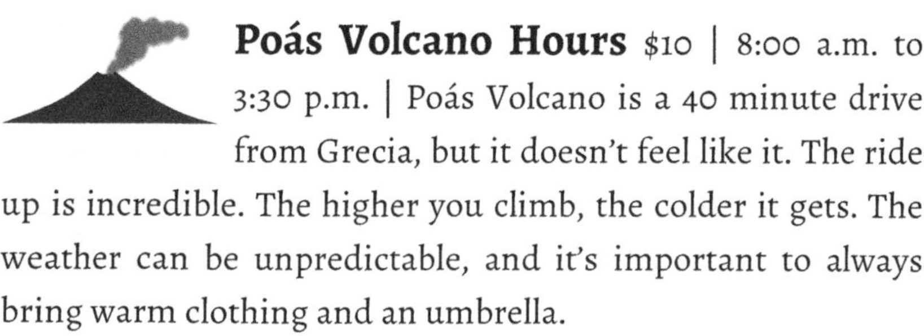

Poás Volcano Hours $10 | 8:00 a.m. to 3:30 p.m. | Poás Volcano is a 40 minute drive from Grecia, but it doesn't feel like it. The ride up is incredible. The higher you climb, the colder it gets. The weather can be unpredictable, and it's important to always bring warm clothing and an umbrella.

Imagine standing on top of the world, looking down at a massive aquamarine lagoon steaming with sulfuric acid. And get this: it is 1000 feet deep, making it the deepest volcanic lagoon on earth.

Even though it looks like the most inviting swimming hole you've ever encountered, the water's pH is zero, which means there will be zero left of you if you decide to swan-dive into it. Occasionally, pressure builds up, causing steam to shoot over 800 feet into the air.

The best time to see Poás Volcano is early in the morning because of less cloud cover.

The trail to the crater is paved and wheelchair accessible. The walk up feels mysterious, with vegetation so verdant it will remind you of *Jurassic Park*. You'll come across a big plant nicknamed the Poor Man's Umbrella. This species is closely related to giant rhubarb, and its leaves are so large, they can easily shelter you from the rain.

Once you're done viewing the crater, you can walk down the trail to Lake Botos. It was a volcanic crater which is now a beautiful lagoon surrounded by lush vegetation. Dozens of hummingbirds dart in front of your face as you hike. Over 80 species of birds call this area home. You'll also notice that plenty of orchids and colorful flowers brighten the path.

Before leaving the park, check out its café and souvenir shop. It's the perfect stop for a hot cup of cocoa. They also have a large-screen projection television where you can learn about the history of the volcano and its various eruptions.

I remember riding our scooter up to Poás and feeling a sense of freedom. It was at a time when I was still unsure of our move and feared how my future would unfold. But it's amazing what a volcano can do for your disposition. Nature has a way of pulling you into its magic. It's hard to have anxiety or feel depressed when you are standing on top of a volcano.

After an excursion to Poás, you can have breakfast at one of the miradors along the mountain ridge just below the entrance. Mirador means "balcony" or "viewpoint" in Spanish. They're often perched high on a ridge with stupendous views. You will come across many while driving throughout Costa Rica, and I urge you to stop at one. But make sure you bring your luggage inside with you; lesson one in avoiding crime.

La Paz Waterfall Gardens Adults $44, Children (3-12) $28 | 8:00 a.m. to 5:00 p.m. | www.waterfallgardens.com |

If you still have time after your stop at the mirador, another fun thing to see is La Paz Waterfall Gardens. It's on the southern side of Poás Volcano and is worth the admission price. On the way, you will drive through rolling hillsides. It's one reason this area is called the Switzerland of Central America. You'll pass cows grazing in Kelly-green pastures and people selling strawberries on the roadside. The weather can be so cool and foggy it may be hard to believe you're still in Costa Rica. On other days, it can be so sunny you can't imagine there was ever a cloud in this sky.

There are five spectacular waterfalls and many exhibits to explore. My favorites are the huge butterfly garden and the free-range frog exhibit. It's here where you'll see colorful leaf and poisonous blue-jeans frogs. It's worth every penny.

A large aviary houses toucans, scarlet macaws, and painted buntings. If you are a bird lover, this is an excellent place to see many species. It's always more fun to observe them in the wild, but La Paz Waterfall Gardens does an excellent job of caring for these birds while making it a great experience for their visitors.

It is important to note that many of the animals at La Paz Waterfall Gardens were donated by MINAE, the Costa Rican Ministry of Wildlife, and were confiscated from people who held them illegally. Their website states: "In many cases the animals were abused and in near-death condition when we received them. We have rehabilitated them and combined them into sociable groups where they have become families." It's unfortunate, but these animals now rely on humans to survive, and it would be dangerous for them if they were released them into the wild.

When you're done viewing La Paz's exhibits, end your day by exploring their five waterfalls. It will require a decent level of fitness. There are metal stairs that are often wet, so it's important to watch your step and take it slow. Platforms are built alongside the waterfalls and are wonderful places to stop for pictures.

If you feel like spending the night, the Peace Lodge is located inside the park. It's pricey but incredibly luxurious.

Link:

Poás Volcano Information: http://en.wikipedia.org/wiki/Poás_Volcano

Great Blue
Heron

San José One-Day Itinerary

When we first moved to Costa Rica, there were no street signs, anywhere in the country. Not even in San José, the capital of Costa Rica. "What a strange thing," I thought. Almost as strange as saying my address is two hundred meters past the old mango tree.

San José now has street signs! A feat that should garner a ticker-tape parade, but the procession's path won't be a straight line. Even with the new signs, this city is still very confusing. I'll be sure to join in, waving my Costa Rican flag and taking selfies at the intersection of Calle 3 and Avenida 0.

Many people fly into San José and stay one night before beginning their tour of the country. Don't waste this valuable Pura Vida time! Call Daniel, our San José driver, to show you around. He was kind enough to share the perfect itinerary for anyone stuck in San José.

"There are a lot of places for you to visit in the main metropolitan area, and we can see most of them in a day," Daniel said. "Short trips like the aerial tram inside the tropical forest of the Zurqui mountain, or a visit to La Paz Waterfall Gardens in the slope of the Poás Volcano. A road trip to waterfall Las Musas in San Ramón and back through Sarchi's furniture and oxcart factories, Grecia's metal church and many beautiful roads with peaceful, breathtaking landscapes.

"I have always told people that the real beauty of Costa Rica is out of the city. Still, some people prefer to experience a day in the San José area. We'll drive through downtown Alajuela and learn about the quest of 1856. In this year, we had to defend our freedom against filibusters, and this province is the cradle of our national hero, Juan Santamaría.

"We'll continue toward the City of the Flowers, Heredia. Here we'll enjoy a delicious *granizado* (similar to a snow cone) while sitting on the old benches of its central park. And for coffee lovers, we can take a tour of the world-famous Britt coffee factory.

"Afterward, we'll visit the city of San José, where the old and the new mix in a cultural scenario that marvels even the seasoned traveler. If they feel like walking, I'll park and introduce them to the pedestrian boulevard of main avenue. We'll see several museums and historical sites like Democracy Plaza, where our army was abolished in 1948. We'll visit Plaza of the Culture as well as the National Theatre and Metropolitan Cathedral.

"We can walk inside the central market and have a good inexpensive meal, the Costa Rican way, in one of the small sodas (mini restaurants). This metropolis offers many options. Places with a long history, like Soda Chelles at the end of the main boulevard or Mi Tierrita (my little land) in the south corner of the National Museum, are just a humble introduction to our typical cuisine.

"After a good meal, we'll visit the artisans market, where you can find all kinds of souvenirs, shirts and Costa Rican items that are a good reminder of this little piece of ground that has found grace in the eyes of the creator. Hopefully, we will have the chance to meet some of the most famous characters of the city during our visit."

Daniel loves his country, and after a day trip with him, you'll know why local people are so proud of what they have accomplished in this little gem called Costa Rica.

Daniel Campos
www.facebook.com/TrueDriverCostaRica
Email: yoamocostarica@gmail.com

Sugar Beach

Guanacaste

"My life is like a stroll on the beach... as near to the edge as I can go."

~ Henry David Thoreau

Guanacaste province is located in the northwest portion of the country and is known as the Gold Coast. Depending on traffic, it takes about five hours to drive from San José. Keep in mind that although Costa Rica is a small country, there are not always direct roads to every destination. It will usually take longer than you think to travel across the country. But these trips aren't like driving down the New Jersey Turnpike. The scenery outside your window is breathtaking.

Guanacaste is the driest part of the country. If you don't like a lot of rain, then this is the place for you. Liberia's international airport is only an hour away from some of the most beautiful beaches. Consider flying into this airport if you plan on visiting this part of the country. I love driving, but sometimes it's nice to fly and arrive precisely at your destination.

The Guanacaste Mountain Range includes four volcanoes: Miravalles, Orosi, Tenorio, and Rincón de la Vieja.

Rincón de la Vieja National Park $15 Adults, $5 Children 6-12 | (Pailas Sector) Tuesday through Sunday, 7:00 a.m. to 3:00 p.m. | Located 16 miles northeast of Liberia, this park is a must-see when visiting Guanacaste. It pretty much has it all: seven hiking trails, rivers, waterfalls, fumaroles, and bubbling mud pots!

Rincón de la Vieja Adventure Tours $92 Adults, $87 Children 13–17 years, $82 Children 4–12 | www.guachipelin.com | If you want to have a fantastic full-day adventure with your family, I would recommend the one-day pass at Adventure Tours. It includes river tubing, horseback riding, hot springs, a volcanic mud bath, a butterfly garden, a serpentarium, a frog exhibit, and zip lining.

THE BEACHES

Playa Hermosa is a beach town about a half hour from the Liberia Airport. Don't confuse it with the other Playa Hermosa near Jacó. This happens often in Costa Rica: there are usually two, three, or four towns with the same name, so make sure when booking your trip that you are heading toward your intended destination. Surrounded by lush vegetation, this beach stretches for over a mile. North of Playa Hermosa is the Gulf of Papagayo, a great place if you like to fish, scuba dive, surf, or snorkel. (Check out the YouTube video URL, at the end of this chapter, of a time lapse we shot there.)

Santa Rosa National Park $15 Adults, $5 Children | 8:00 a.m. to 3:30 p.m. | Santa Rosa is Costa Rica's first national park and is home to 250 species of birds, including the white-tailed hawk, the ivory-billed woodcreeper, and the Pacific screech owl.

In between bird-watching, keep an eye out for white-faced and spider monkeys, ocelots, and anteaters. And just in case you are looking for bats, there are plenty here, including the "vampire" species. I have no idea what to make of that, but I'm sure I'll be face to face with one someday since I have an uncanny ability for exploring caves while simultaneously falling into piles of bat crap. It's a graceful talent, skillfully perfected after years of participating in my husband's economical two-for-one excursions.

If you're renting a good four-wheel-drive vehicle, drive down to Playa Naranjo and look out at Witch's Rock, a popular surfing destination. It has a majestic quality, rising out of the ocean, almost daring you to come and surf its waters.

Playa del Coco Travel a little farther south and you'll hit Coco, a popular destination for both expats and tourists. Here you'll find restaurants, casinos, nightlife, and shopping. There will also be lots of people walking up to you and offering tours. This is where many people charter fishing trips or set out for scuba diving. Surfers can also catch a boat to Witch's Rock from here.

Rob went on a fishing trip out of Playa del Coco and caught jacks and red snapper. Inshore fishing trips can range from $350 to $650 for half- or full-day tours. If you're interested in offshore deep sea fishing, chartering a boat will cost approximately $600 for a half-day trip and $1,200 for a full-day trip. Prices change depending on the time of year.

Images of this town, a fishing trip out of Playa del Coco, and my delicious red snapper recipe can be seen in a video we did (URL at end of chapter)!

Dream On Sportfishing Tel: 8735-3121 | www.dreamonsportfishing.com | If you're interested in an awesome day out on the water, call Rick at Dream On.

Playa Ocotal Only five minutes away from Playa del Coco is Playa Ocotal. It's a calm beach perfect for relaxing or snorkeling. Where there are rocky outcroppings, there are usually interesting fish. Be sure to explore these tide pools while visiting this area.

Diamante Eco Adventure Park Tel: 2105-5200 | www.diamanteecoadventurepark.com | Adventure Pass: $118 Adults, $95 Children | Stop by this park and spend a fun-filled day zip-lining, Atv-ing, paddle boarding, kayaking, and horseback riding. Enjoy their animal sanctuary, home to frogs, snakes, crocodiles, monkeys, sloths, beautiful birds, a butterfly observatory and a variety of cats, including pumas and jaguars.

Playa Danta Two of my favorite beaches south from Playa Ocotal are Playa Danta and its little sister, Playa Danita. These beaches are best accessed from my area, Playa Flamingo. You can also get here using the Congo trail from Playa Ocotal. When the dirt road is in good shape, it will take 45 minutes. It is important to check road conditions since the trail washes out often. You can also travel on paved roads, through Belen, which takes about an hour and 15 minutes.

It's here at Playa Danta that you'll find the Las Catalinas development—the same place where we filmed the cocktail scene from our EX-PATS episode with Savannah Buffett (Jimmy Buffett's daughter). You can find this production on the Reserve Channel on YouTube. If you're the adventurous type, grab a bite at their restaurant before checking out Pura Vida Ride (www.puravidaride.com) to rent kayaks, paddleboards, and mountain bikes.

Sentido Norte Restaurant Tel: 2103 1200 | www.sentidonorterestaurant.com | This restaurant with its breathtaking views is located between Playa Danta and Sugar Beach. You'll need reservations, and children under 10 are not allowed. I would recommend you go before sunset, sit in their lounge, and watch the best show on earth. You've never seen a sunset like the ones you'll witness in Costa Rica. And this one ends with a fire show!

Sugar Beach I really like this beach, and it's not too far from my home. There is something unique about how it's nestled in a cove. It feels intimate, familiar, a place you'll want to smooch your spouse. The waves are perfect for boogie boarding. I took my mother-in-law to this beach and watched my husband position her on the board before releasing her into oncoming waves. Over, and over, and over again! She screamed like a little girl every time. (She also screamed because the board's leash wrapped around her leg and she thought it was a sea snake. Video URL at end of chapter).

Hotel Sugar Beach Hotel Sugar Beach Tel: 2654-4242 www.sugar-beach.com | You'll have to walk through Hotel Sugar Beach to get down to the ocean. It's the perfect place to stop for a cold drink or enjoy their restaurant after playing in the sea. The touristy town of Tamarindo is fun, but for those on a honeymoon—or just wanting to get away from it all—Hotel Sugar Beach is very romantic. The restaurant is an excellent place to watch the sun set over the water while enjoying great food and friendly service. You might even catch me here, drinking an Orange Fanta and working on my next book.

Sugar Beach is one of the best beaches in the area to boogie board, but make sure to stay in its center to avoid rocks.

"Time you enjoy wasting is not wasted time."
~ Marthe Troly-Curtin

Playa Prieta is a secret little beach easy to miss. It's south of Sugar Beach, and you must keep an eye out for a steep road pointing down towards the ocean. I must have driven past this for two years before realizing it even existed.

Once you're at the ocean, you'll see little bungalows bordering the beach. It's always so peaceful here and never crowded. In fact, I don't remember ever seeing more than a few people. Because of this, it's a bird-watcher's dream.

We once observed a great blue heron staring down at us from an overhead branch. Over three feet tall, he closely followed our movements and never let us out of his sight. It felt like walking past one of those portraits whose eyes follow you around the room.

A great blue heron's distinct call sounds a lot like a duck with laryngitis. I know this because the bird let out a vociferous belch. He was either about to peck our eyes out or warning us to stop tramping through his all-you-can-eat buffet. Apparently, we walked through a bunch of purple and orange Halloween crabs that subsequently darted into the sand. You'll see these crabs throughout Costa Rica, and you can usually find them at the base of trees on many beaches.

Playa Penca This was one of the first beaches I visited in Costa Rica. It is also the place where I said, "You know what? I want to move here. I'm all in." I couldn't imagine never seeing this place again.

To find Playa Penca, look for a road right next to a tiny strip of stores in Potrero, just around the soccer field. Turn down this dirt path, and it will take you straight to the beach. Playa

Penca has soft white sand that cradles your feet like warm slippers. It's a great place to roll out your towel, relax, and watch the ocean sparkle. It's like someone has scattered silver glitter across the waves.

There are outcroppings of rocks on the north end of the beach. I wouldn't recommend swimming out to them, but if you can find yourself a kayak, this is a great place to snorkel. Unfortunately, there isn't a place to rent kayaks on this beach, but keep this spot in mind. This is one of those "in the know" places that locals talk about.

Playa Potrero is a long stretch of beach where many people take their daily walks. My friend Richard, when not fixing his ice maker, catches fish here, and it's not uncommon to see men walking up and down this stretch of sands with fishing poles.

Since this beach is next to a few hotels and restaurants, it's a nice place to stay for a few days.

El Castillo Tel: 2573-4233 | You can't miss this place! It'll be the castle on the corner. Locals go there for their excellent steaks, cheesecake, and all kinds of delicious food.

Cerveceria Independiente http://independiente.cr If you like good beer, stop by this brewery located only blocks from the beach. The owners are fun and they make some of the best beer in all of Costa Rica.

Perla's http://perlas.pub | Perla's has a big-screen bar atmosphere and an eclectic menu and is very popular with the locals. They're known for their perogies, but they're not always on the menu.

The Shack | www.facebook.com/TheShackCR | A fun place to enjoy live music and a cold beer. Their banana macadamia nut pancakes are to die for!

Maxwell's Café and Bar |www.facebook.com/Fresh-FoodatKellys | You'll find many local people here. There are known in the area for serving breakfast throughout the day. If you are looking to meet other expats, while enjoying a great meal, stop by.

Smokin' Pig Tel: 2654-4545 | www.facebook.com/smokinpigcr | If you're looking for ribs, brisket, and pecan pie, this is the place for you! Southern-style barbecue just blocks away from the ocean. Could you ask for more?

Playa Flamingo is the crown jewel of my local beaches, perfectly positioned in a cove with incredible houses peering down from the ridges. Here you will find Margaritaville Beach Resort. It's just across the road from the beach. They rent small boats and Jet Skis here. There's a shopping center within walking distance that includes a pharmacy, a rental car agency, and the famous Marie's Restaurant.

Marie's Restaurant Tel: 2654-4136 | Marie is an actual person and has lived in this area since long before there was much of anything else here. She is a really fun lady, and you might even get the chance to see her there, working the bar or assisting her waiters. Any story I have about Costa Rica, she has a better one. I could write a whole book just on her. Rob and I remember going to her restaurant before there was a shopping center. Giant iguanas and magpies would chase customers around for French fries and sugar packets.

Coco Loco Tel: 2654-6242 | Coco Loco is located right on the sand just a short distance from Flamingo Beach Resort. The chef is one of the best in the area. The drinks are not only delicious but also beautifully presented. After you drink an alcoholic beverage out of a coconut, you'll want to call your boss and tell him you're not coming back to work. Make sure to shut off your phone if you can't afford to quit your job.

Margaritaville Beach Resort Tel: 844-569-8851 www.margaritavillebeachresortcostarica.com | This hotel has replaced the Flamingo Beach Resort and is the most prominent hotel on the beach.

Paradise Flamingo Beach Tel: 2654-4311 | www.paradiseflamingobeach.com | This hotel is a real find and has one of the best views in the area. It's an older hotel that is currently being upgraded, but you can't beat the location. I notice this often in Costa Rica; many older hotels have the best spots.

Playa Brasilito A quiet little beach town, very close to my home. A variety of souvenir shops surround its soccer field, as well as several small sodas. Be sure to check them out for an economical meal. It's not uncommon to see people making out in the ocean. They should have named this place the kissing beach.

Soda Brasilito is located here and is a very popular place to eat with the locals. Another great place to watch the sunset is at Gracia within the Mar Vista residential development. This restaurant has great views and excellent food. You can even jump into their infinity pool while waiting for your meal. The chef, Frankie, always walks out wearing a fedora and talks with everyone. He's so friendly and adorable, you'll want to return another day just to talk to him again. This restaurant is within walking distance of The Happier House.

Soda Brasilito Maybe the most popular soda in the area. They stay busy most of the year and are the perfect stop for an affordable meal. And you're right across from the beach!

Gracia Tel: 6110-1687 | www.graciamarvista.com | You must try Frankie's crispy cauliflower and sesame soy ahi. He really knows how to cook! Sometimes you meet a chef who's really giving it his all and loves his craft. Frankie is that guy.

Lucy's Retired Surfers Bar & Restaurant
Tel: 8529-4438 | www.lucysretiredsurfers.com/costarica
Lucy's is across the road from Brasilito Beach and known for being a fun place to have lunch or a cocktail. I love their burgers! And if you're in the mood to do their famous scorpion shot, you can

go home with a T-shirt. You read that right: a shot with an actual scorpion in it! Now that comes with some bragging rights.

Oasis Restaurant | www.facebook.com/eloasisbrasilito Another restaurant I enjoy in Brasilito is Oasis. Facing the ocean, they serve great seafood dishes and prepare an excellent red snapper. Don't be surprised to see a happy dog at your feet here or at any other beachfront restaurant for that matter. They patiently wait for something to fall to the ground, and when you're done, they go on to the next table. They are not monogamous at all with their begging.

Hotel Brasilito Tel: 2654-4237 | www.brasilito.com | If you're looking for something bare-boned and super affordable, this is the place. Located just across a sandy road from the beach.

Playa Conchal Right next door to Playa Brasilito is Playa Conchal, one of the more popular beaches in the entire area. We love it and our guests do, too. It's also the home to the Reserva Conchal development (which includes the Westin Hotel). I have a friend who lives there, and whenever I visit, I go straight to the spa and jump into their enormous hot tub. It's like something straight out of Nero's palace. And when I'm looking to exercise, their treadmills have incredible views of the ocean. I find that I'm more motivated to burn off calories when I'm watching passing sailboats. Reserva Conchal is like a fantasy camp for adults.

You used to be able to drive to this beach, but due to environmental concerns, this is no longer possible. You must now park around the Brasilito soccer field and walk approximately twenty minutes south. Most of the vendors that were once on this beach, you can now find on Playa Penca.

There is an excellent reef not too far offshore that's perfect for snorkeling. It's not uncommon to find families of howler monkeys here.

Westin Playa Conchal Resort and Spa Tel: 2654-3500 www.marriott.com | If you're looking for all-inclusive luxury, the Westin certainly delivers. They have over ten restaurants and every amenity you can imagine. You can book your excursions here and have easy access to Playa Conchal. Reserva Conchal golf course is located here.

Conchal Hotel Tel: 2654-9125 | www.conchalcr.com | A great hotel run by attentive owners. It's also a good choice if you're on a budget. Their Papaya restaurant is one of the best in the area.

Playa Puerto Viejo This beach is attached to Playa Conchal at the far end, but it's a long walk. While it's relatively close as the crow flies, it's off the beaten path when you're trying to get there by car. The drive makes you feel like you're deep in the jungle. It's common to see monkeys and other animals here. It offers some of the best snorkeling in the area. In low tide, you can walk across the rocks on a calm day and find many coral reefs.

We filmed one of our underwater videos here , and Rob got an up-close view of an inking octopus (video URL at end of chapter). You can also kayak over to the protruding rocks and watch for manta rays breaching the surface. They leap out of the sea like UFOs, the tips of their fins catching the reflection of the sun. And just as quickly, they dive back into the ocean, transforming into shadowy creatures lurking under your kayak.

Two other interesting beaches close by are Minas and Pirates Bay. You can find an outcropping on Pirate Bay with a cave inside! It's rumored that Captain Morgan stashed his rum and treasure here. Rob convinced me to walk out at low tide and scale the rock in search of gold. We uncovered the cave, saw lots of bats, and fell in guano, but no rum was found. Which I could have used at that point.

Playa Grande The town of Matapalo is a good reference point when searching for Puerto Viejo or Playa Grande. If you drive fifteen minutes south from the town's soccer field, you'll find Playa Grande and Ventanas. These beaches are situated within Las Baulas National Park, an area where leatherback turtles nest. The hatching season is October through May, and if you're lucky, you might get a chance to see one lay her eggs.

Leatherbacks are the world's largest turtles, weighing close to 1200 pounds, and they can be nearly seven feet in length. Although they have survived for 150 million years, they are now decreasing in number. Great efforts have been made by the Playa Grande community to help preserve these turtles. Small tours can be arranged with licensed guides to witness them laying their eggs on the beach. No lights or camera flashes are permitted, and the guides stress that you should not get too close to the mother turtles.

Watching a turtle lay her eggs and return to the sea is the experience of a lifetime. It will change how you see our environment, and it made me realize how much of this planet is connected in such miraculous ways. It's the reason I always suggest venturing away from hotels and thoroughly exploring an area. The most incredible places exist just minutes from touristy towns, often at the end of bumpy dirt roads.

If you're a surfer, look no further. Playa Grande offers consistent breaks and swells. It's among the best surfing locations in the entire country, but be very careful swimming here. I've personally experienced strong riptides, one of which nearly sucked my mother-in-law out to sea. After my husband brought her back to shore, she yelled at him, wanting to go back out again.

As you enter Playa Grande, you'll find an attendant wearing a reflective vest standing in front of a parking lot. I believe he charges two dollars, and I would suggest you park here leaving nothing in your car.

To your right are a couple of picnic benches and a food stand. It's the perfect spot to grab a cool drink and watch the surfers. You can also enjoy a meal at the neighboring Hotel Las Tortugas. The owner has done much to preserve the leatherbacks' habitat, so go on in and buy a soda or a plate of nachos. It's the least we can do to reward his efforts in making this world a better place. To learn more about him, be sure to check out his EX-PATS episode on the Reserve Channel on YouTube.

Hotel Las Tortugas Tel: 2653-0423 | www.lastortugashotel.net | If you are a surfer, or just enjoy waking up steps away from the ocean, you'll love this hotel.

Playa Ventanas There is more shade on this beach, and fewer people. Where I grew up in New Jersey, the beaches were always crowded. Now I love the feeling of wading in the water and not having to overhear how Joey Ravioli drank fifteen tequila shots at the club last night.

The ocean is calmer at this beach, and it's where Rob tries to surf. I would show you pictures of my husband surfing, but it's hard to get a good shot since he spends a majority of his time on the ocean floor. He now sticks to boogie boarding.

During low tide, it's fun to explore the many tide pools. They're filled with all sorts of fish and coral. One can easily wander around for hours examining the interesting sea life. Look for me here in my big-brimmed hat, pointing at sea urchins. I have many memories of walking along this beach with my husband.

Tamarindo One of the most popular places in Costa Rica, and not far from The Happier House, Tamarindo is known for surfing and nightlife. But you don't have to surf to enjoy this spot. The road into town ends in a circle where you can park and do a little shopping or people watching. One of our favorite things to do is eat lunch at the Tamarindo Diria Beach Resort. We once watched a dog surf the waves all afternoon. It's also a place where we've filmed some of the most spectacular sunsets.

If you're looking for gifts, this is souvenir heaven. Vendors sell beautiful jewelry at stands set up all alongside the street, and there's one souvenir shop after the other. The craftsmanship is incredible, and many pieces are reasonably priced.

After exploring Tamarindo, you may want to relax on a less-crowded beach. No problem. I have a general rule for this:

Travel ten minutes north or south from a busy beach, and you'll likely find one that's completely deserted.

I can't stress enough how much fun it is to get out and explore the area. Take excursions or hire a taxi driver to show you around. It's worth the money, and you will find that all the magical things that people love so dearly about Costa Rica are often just a couple of minutes from the main attractions.

Hotel Capitán Suizo Tel: 2653-0075 | www.hotelcapitansuizo.com | Still one of the most popular boutique hotels in Tamarindo, Hotel Capitán Suizo sits steps away from the ocean. It's on the road toward Langosta.

Esplendor Tamarindo Tel: 4700-4747 | www.wyndhamtamarindo.com/en | What a view! What a pool! Although this hotel is not on the beach, it makes up for it with a vista that anyone would want to wake up to. If you don't stay here, I would recommend stopping by for dinner or a cocktail. You won't be disappointed.

Hotel Pasatiempo Tel: 2653-0028 | www.hotelpasatiempo.com | Nice affordable hotel with a great vibe. The bungalows are adorable, and your family will feel right at home here. It's only a five-minute walk to the beach!

La Palapa www.palapacr.com | Rob and I love this restaurant! He always gets the fish and chips, while I get the Cajun blackened tuna. It's right on the sand, and at night they often have a fire show.

Pangas Beach Club http://pangasbeachclubcr.com Stop by this beautiful restaurant on your way into Tamarindo. If you're thinking about a wedding or large get-together, I would certainly choose this place. Try their Guanacaste Sampler, enjoy the ocean breeze, and forget about your worries.

Playa Avellanas Travel about 15 minutes south from Tamarindo, onto a dirt road, and you'll hit Playa Avellanas, a great beach for surfing and boogie boarding

Lola's Restaurant www.facebook.com/playaavellana A popular place to relax, stick your toes in the sand, and enjoy lunch. It's named after their pet pig, which may be more famous than the actual restaurant!

JW Marriott Tel: 888-236-2427 | www.jwguanacastespa.com | Situated right on the beach, this resort is a playground for families. The rooms wrap around a massive pool that overlooks the ocean. There are seven restaurants, a spa, and all kinds of water sports equipment. Note: The beach area is rocky and can have strong rip-tides.

Playa Negra A 10-minute drive further south on a dirt road from Avellanas is Playa Negra. The entrance is one of the prettiest I've seen. A canopy of mango trees shades a cobblestone path before leading you onto the sand. One area of this beach is great for experienced surfers, while another has smaller waves perfect for intermediate surfers and boogie-boarders. We catch awesome waves here, and the beach is rarely crowded.

Playa Ostional It's approximately an hour and a half drive from Tamarindo. Although an adventurous journey, I certainly suggest it. I highly recommend a four-wheel-drive vehicle for this trip. Imagine thousands of mother turtles swimming toward the beach, their heads jutting out of the water like submarine periscopes. Once the turtles get to shore, their flippers propel them forward, inch by inch, in search of the perfect spot to lay their eggs. I've never witnessed anything more beautiful.

Playa Ostional is one of the world's most important nesting sites for Olive Ridley turtles. The nesting season is usually between August and November. It starts with a few hundred turtles, and later thousands upon thousands come ashore (in what is known as the "arribada"). It's nothing short of amazing.

After laying their eggs, these mothers must struggle back to the ocean. With every step forward, they stop and take a huge breath. They're exhausted, but little by little, they continue onward. Their flippers aren't designed for trudging through sand, so it can take them hours before they finally reach the water's edge. But once they do, they quickly disappear into the ocean.

Their babies hatch between 45 and 55 days later. They must dig their way up to the surface and follow the moonlight toward the surf. It's a harrowing race: vultures await. Even if they're lucky enough to make it past the birds, more predators are hiding in the ocean.

This land race is extremely important for the baby turtles. Their movements help develop and open their tiny lungs. Because of this, you shouldn't pick them up and take them to the water. But you can protect them from the vultures overhead. It was during one of these arribadas that Rob untangled a turtle from a fishing net. No one had a knife, so Rob diligently ripped the net apart with his own hands. (Video URL at end of chapter.)

Hotel Luna Azul Tel: 2682-1400 | www.hotellunaazul.com Nobody knows more about the turtles than the owners at Luna Azul. They always let me know when the arribada begins. Their hotel sits high on a ridge and has an incredible view of the ocean. The breakfasts are amazing, and the owner even makes his own jellies!

Nosara A short drive from Playa Ostional, Nosara is a quiet community nestled under shady trees and is one of the prettiest towns in all of Costa Rica. "Happy molecules" float in the air, and their beaches, Guiones and Pelada, are perfect gems. You'll want to bury your feet in the sand and dream about running away forever.

Getting to Nosara can be tricky: there are a few rivers to drive through. During the rainy season, these rivers can be difficult to cross, so be careful. I always recommend four-wheel drive.

Samara Just an hour south of Nosara is the adorable town of Samara. It comprises only a few blocks, but it has that nice slow pace Costa Rica is known for. Carrillo beach is less than five miles away and is picture perfect. Whoever designed this area should be given an award. The road is lined with palm trees and looks like a movie set.

It feels as if you can walk out forever into the surf without the water ever getting above your waist. Rob and I once walked out so far, I turned around and was shocked to see how far off in the distance the shore was. It's a special place and worth visiting.

Nicoya Peninsula

If you want to get away from it all, travel the back roads from Samara all the way down the Nicoya Peninsula. It gets better and better the farther you go, but be aware, this peninsula becomes very remote. Don't be surprised if you see vans full of surfers on the road—they always know where to find the best beaches.

Santa Teresa and Mal País are two popular locations at the tip of the peninsula (not Guanacaste, but

Puntarenas Province). These places would make for the perfect honeymoon. No crowds, lots of wildlife, and incredible sunsets.

Blue Surf Sanctuary Tel: 2640-1001 | www.bluesurf-sanctuary.com | A great place to unwind, do yoga, or surf.

I hope you enjoyed this literary tour of Guanacaste. It was fun showing you around the many beaches I visit. Maybe now you understand why I'm so happy here. It's near impossible to get bored. If I ever start feeling antsy, Rob and I just hop in the car and start exploring.

Links:

Playa Hermosa Time Lapse: https://youtu.be/uVhLL1r0yxs
Playa de Coco Fishing Trip: https://youtu.be/WJcwiLqV0B0
Savannah Buffett Show: https://youtu.be/ord0JeMPC7Q
Underwater Video: https://youtu.be/ndV9uBSKKI0
Tamarindo Time Lapse: https://youtu.be/GivU5LdEc0U
Turtle Invasion: https://youtu.be/UF5s0qN8CWU
Rob Saving Turtle: https://youtu.be/c1lmB32Uw7M

Arenal & Monteverde

"I can't control the wind but I can adjust the sail."
~ Ricky Skaggs

Arenal

The Garden of Eden—that's the best way to describe Arenal and the surrounding La Fortuna area. You'll find primary rainforests, canyons, hanging bridges, waterfalls, and an abundance of wildlife. With moderate temperatures compared to the beach, it's no wonder so many expats call it home.

Inhale a deep breath of this magical air while hiking through the forest. Little vegetation grows on the forest floor due to the thick canopy overhead that prevents sunlight from reaching the ground. It's spooky yet fascinating, and this forest hasn't changed in a million years. It's a place unlike any other and is worthy of a road trip.

If you're traveling from the San José Airport, it's about a three-hour ride. You'll arrive on the eastern side of the lake in the touristy town of La Fortuna. From Guanacaste, it's approximately a two-hour ride, and you'll arrive on the western side of Lake Arenal. It's another hour drive around the lake from here to get to the volcano and La Fortuna.

The word "majestic" comes to mind when describing Arenal Volcano. It's a young one, less than 7,500 years old. A baby when compared to other volcanoes. When it was active, people would flock there to watch molten boulders exploding into the night sky. In 2010, Arenal Volcano entered a quiet phase, so it's no longer erupting but could start up again at any time. Active or inactive, this area is worth the trip.

Arenal National Park $15 | 8:00 a.m. to 3:00 p.m. | If you had to choose one trail to hike, I would pick the 1.24-mile Lava Flow Trail (Sendero Coladas). It wraps around the base of the volcano, and you'll cross the lava beds from Arenal's 1992 eruption. Keep your camera handy, since you're likely to see many exotic birds and all sorts of wildlife.

Arenal Observatory Lodge Tel: 2290-7011 | www.arenalobservatorylodge.com | This is my favorite place to stay in Arenal. Located at the base of the volcano in the town of El Castillo, it has views that will knock your socks off. Every morning you'll witness magnificent Montezuma oropendolas flying down to eat fruit supplied by this hotel. Coatis waddle around while toucans hover above, watching the action. It's a scene straight from a wilderness movie. There are also many amazing hiking trails, so you don't have to even leave the hotel grounds to experience the wonders of the area. This is where an ocelot jumped on my husband's back. This picture is not photoshopped as some people have suggested!

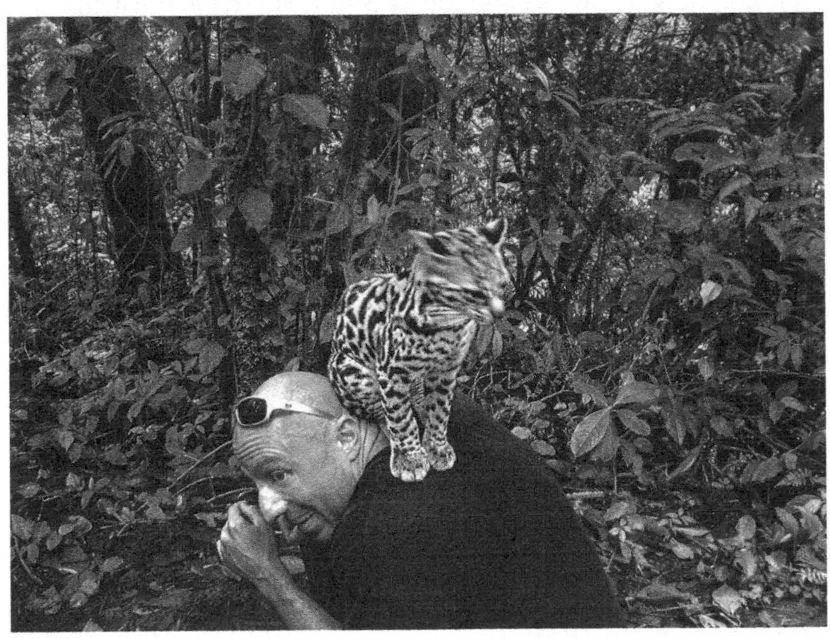

Fun Fact: Fun Fact: It's hard to comprehend how a toucan can fly with such a huge bill. However, it turns out its bill doesn't weigh much at all. It's filled with honeycombed bone, allowing air to flow through. This acts as the bird's personal thermostat and regulates body heat. They also use it as a fencing sword, wrestling their neighbors to show dominance. But what I like most about toucans is their mating ritual: their foreplay consists of tossing fruit at one another. It looks fun and seems like an excellent way to enjoy snacks while getting frisky.

Tabacón Grand Spa Thermal Resort Tel: 2479-2099 www.tabacon.com | This hotel is popular for its hot springs. If you choose not to stay here, you can still buy a day pass and enjoy a luxurious day. Although this a wonderful way to relax, be sure to ask the locals about the free, naturally occurring hot springs down the road.

Gingerbread Restaurant Tel: 2694-0039 www.gingerbreadarenal.com | As you drive around the lake, you'll come across the Gingerbread Restaurant about five minutes from Nuevo Arenal, famous for some of the best food in the area.

Mystica Tel: 2692-1001 | www.mysticacostarica.com | When you just need a great slice of pizza, served by friendly staff. As simple as that.

Essence Arenal Tel: 2479-1131 | www.essencearenal.com | This remarkable hostel and organic farm is situated on top of a hill overlooking the volcano. Niko, the owner, is committed to living a sustainable lifestyle and has carried this vision over into his business. Don't be surprised when you're greeted by free-range chickens, ones that will never become your dinner! This is a vegetarian establishment.

Take a tour of his farm and his edible entryway, and explore the rows of mixed-crop vegetables planted to deter insects. There is even a coffee field. The yoga platform overlooks Arenal volcano, and it's here you'll experience a different frequency running through your body. This happens to me often in Costa

Rica; I'm so at peace that my eyes widen a bit more, appreciating this beautiful planet.

Essence Arenal has several types of rooms to choose from: bedrooms with private baths, tents with a shared bathroom, or if you're budget-minded, you can even camp on their grounds. There are cooking demonstrations in the evening, where guests all take part in preparing a vegetarian dish. This place may have the coolest vibe of anywhere I've traveled in Costa Rica. (Video URL of our interview with Nikko at end of chapter.)

Rancho Margot Tel: 8302-7318 | www.ranchomargot.com
I've said this before: the best things in Costa Rica are usually down a dirt road. Rancho Margot is the brainchild of Juan Sostheim, a retired fast-food executive whose initial intention was to run a ranch that would be carbon-neutral. He has done much more than that: his ranch is carbon-negative. He's taking green technology and applying it on a large scale.

Rancho Margot grows their own food, builds their own furniture and produces their own electricity. They even make their own soap! I hope you all have time to visit Rancho Margot. Take their tour, or stay for a few days. It will change the way you think. And if you get a chance to meet Juan, ask him to do some sophisticated math. I watched in amazement as he converted kilowatts of electricity into BTUs. I can barely understand how to convert dollars into colones, while Juan does long division in his head. This is a smart guy.

Activities

Sky Adventure Tours Tel: 2479-4100 | www.skyadventures.travel | Starting at $81 for adults, $56 for kids | This outfit is in El Castillo and has been in business for over fifteen years. They have a variety of tours, but their most popular is their zip line and tram ride. The tram takes you up into the canopy, where you can then return via the tram or by zip lining!

They also have a Sky Walk tour: five suspension bridges that span across canyons and take you up into the treetops. It typically takes three hours.

La Fortuna Waterfall (La Catarata Rio Fortuna) $15, Children under 8 free | 7:00 a.m. to 5:00 p.m. | www.catarata-lafortuna.com | Imagine walking down 530 steps through dense forest while hypnotized by the thunderous sound of water. At the bottom, the La Fortuna waterfall rises 230 feet, reminding you that nature's power far supersedes your own. It's advised not to swim too close to the falls due to strong currents. For those who want a calmer experience, there is a lovely swimming hole to the left.

Windsurfing and Kitesurfing www.ticowind.com | Arenal Lake is famous for its kite- and windsurfing. I've watched many people hijack a gust of wind and fly high into the air, only to land back on the lake and continue surfing. You can rent your equipment at Tico Wind. However, they're only open between November and April.

Rafting Tours Rios Tropicales Tel: 2233-6455 | www.riostropicales.com | This company has an experience for every tourist in mind. Offering adrenaline-packed white-water rapids as well as to gentler floats, they'll make sure you'll have incredible memories of Costa Rica.

Butterfly Conservatory $15 cash | 8:30 a.m. to 4:30 p.m. (last tour at 4:00 p.m.) | www.butterflyconservatory.org | Near Arenal Observatory Lodge is one of the largest butterfly conservatories in Costa Rica. This garden has a collection of butterflies that will satisfy any insect lover. You'll see blue morpho butterflies and be amazed by the glass-winged species, a unique insect that lacks colored scales and is transparent.

And for those of you who like amphibians, the Butterfly Conservatory also has a frog exhibit. You'll be treated to some of the most dazzling frogs native to Costa Rica: the green-and-black poison dart frog, strawberry dart frog (blue jeans frog), and the photogenic red-eyed tree frog. You'll see red-eyed tree frogs printed on postcards, paintings, and billboards all throughout the country. In fact, Costa Rica should add him to their currency. He's that pretty.

Cute Fact: Butterflies do not live on nectar alone. They also dine on fermenting fruit, and it's not uncommon for them to get inebriated on the alcohol. Glen, the owner, says that being tipsy helps butterflies elude predators by encouraging erratic flight patterns. Watching drunk butterflies is quickly becoming one of my favorite pastimes. (Video URL of our interview with Glenn at end of chapter.)

Monteverde

I'd like to just get one of those pink clouds and put you in it and push you around. ~ F. Scott Fitzgerald

Do you enjoy clouds? How about clouds and forests together? Well then, you're in luck! Monteverde combines both of these things.

Cloud forests are unique in that they house specific forms of life that have acclimated to the climate. Because of their elevation, warm ocean air travels up the mountains, ultimately creating this remarkable environment. Imagine walking through a lush forest dense in ferns, bromeliads, and orchids. It's the ultimate fairy tale setting, and at times you'll be literally walking through clouds.

For bird lovers, you may never want to leave. Monteverde is home to the elusive resplendent quetzal as well as the bare-necked umbrella. Even if you're unimpressed with birds, it's impossible not to see these beauties and say, "Wow, Hazel. Ain't that something!"

Keep your eyes open for an ocelot or tapir. From bats to jaguars, this cloud forest will ensure that you bring home wonderful memories of Costa Rica.

Getting to Monteverde

If driving from Arenal (a two-and-a-half-hour drive), take Route 142 to Tilaran, and then Route 145 to Route 606. Route 606 is finally getting paved (yay!), so hopefully you'll have a smoother ride than others did in the past. If driving from San

José (a two hour-and-forty-five minute drive), take Route 34 to Highway 1, then onward to Route 606.

It's chilly in Monteverde so pack accordingly. Unfortunately, those flip-flops and bikinis will leave you chilled to the bone.

Hidden Canopy Treehouses www.hiddencanopy.com Do treehouses and luxury go together? Here it does! Enjoy this bed-and-breakfast at an elevation of 5000 feet. You'll have many of the comforts of home while looking out for the elusive resplendent quetzal.

Links:
Nikko Interview: https://youtu.be/Q_kStNtUh6M
Glen Interview: https://youtu.be/DPU-ODldDcs

Manzanillo Rock

Caribbean

"In order to write about life, first you must live it."
~ Ernest Hemingway

Costa Rica's Caribbean shoreline is everything you imagine: palm trees sleepily lean over the road, and ocean breezes affectionately hug your body, promising to wash away your worries. There's something about the tranquil turquoise water that makes people consider never returning home. It's where those crazy ideas take form, like "Hazel, I've been thinking. We can open a hot chocolate stand, right here, across from the beach!" And get this... Hazel will agree.

This area of the country is much more humid and has its share of rain, but it won't bother you while you're surrounded by the lush forest and incredible wildlife. I've seen more sloths here than anywhere else in the country. And when you watch a sloth climb a tree, ever so slowly, you can't imagine wanting to leave.

Getting to the Caribbean

Flying: You can fly with SANSA from the San José airport to Limón. From there, you're about a half hour away from the first major town in this area, Playa Cahuita.

Driving: It's approximately a six-hour drive from San José and a ten-hour drive from Liberia. After passing through San José, turn onto Route 32. It's easy sailing from here. Continue following Route 32 all the way into Limón, then turn right onto Route 36 and travel south down the Caribbean coast.

Now turn off the air conditioning and roll down the windows. Smell that turquoise-blue air. I've found that the happier I've become, the more colors I smell. Nosara's air smells like jungle green, and Sugar Beach smells like canary yellow. My nose can paint a picture no matter where I travel in Costa Rica.

If you are heading toward Tortuguero, turn left once you're at the Port of Limón. Find a safe place to park your car, and then hop aboard a boat destined for the northeastern tip of the country. This area is only accessible by boat or air. More and more tour companies are offering Tortuguero excursion packages, and if it fits your budget, I would highly recommend it. This area is a very important nesting site for the endangered green turtle.

Things You'll See on Your Way!

Braulio Carrillo National Park $12 | 8:00 a.m. to 4:00 p.m. | A beautiful area that has the highest level of ecological diversity in all of Costa Rica. I wouldn't recommend hiking in this park without a guide; there are many cliffs, and it's easy to get lost in the thick vegetation. Seriously, don't do it. People have hiked here and disappeared.

Rainforest Adventure $59 | www.rainforestadventure.com | If your heart is set on exploring Braulio Carrillo Park, Rainforest Adventure offers an aerial tram that gives an excellent bird's-eye view of the forest.

The Port of Limón

Limón traces its roots back to Jamaican and Chinese laborers who worked on a railroad connecting Limon to San José. It's now best known for its port, which is also where cruise ships stop. There's a gas station right at the corner, so gas up here before continuing your journey south.

Sloth Sanctuary Adults, $15 Kids 5–12 | 8:00 a.m. to 2:00 p.m. Tuesday–Sunday | www.slothsanctuary.com | The Sloth Sanctuary is 19 miles (30 km) south of Limón. Look for "sloth crossing" signs.

This sanctuary is home to the three-fingered and two-fingered sloth. Take the Buttercup Tour, meet rescued sloths, and learn all about their behavior. As part of the tour, you'll also take a canoe ride on the Estrella River and experience the lush vegetation of the tropical rainforest.

Cute Facts: Three-fingered sloths have nine cervical vertebrae instead of the typical seven most other mammals possess. This allows them to rotate their head three hundred degrees to scan for predators without wasting energy turning their bodies.

Sloths never have a good hair day because it grows in the opposite direction as compared to other animals. This follicle arrangement helps protect them from the environment while they hang upside down. The smile on their faces and peculiar movements makes them one of the most adorable animals in Costa Rica.

Beaches

Cahuita About a half hour south of Limón, you will see the small town of Cahuita, home to a beautiful park.

Cahuita National Park Donation at Main Entrance or $5 at the Puerto Vargas Sector | I would certainly visit this magnificent park. You'll glimpse white-faced monkeys, howlers, sloths, and a variety of other animals. If you see something running on water, that's a Jesus Christ lizard! Butterflies surround you while two types of toucans (the chestnut-mandibled and the keel-billed) dart overhead.

I've seen the most spectacular wildlife on rainy days, so don't let bad weather stop you from exploring. Pack a rain hat, one that's not attached to a poncho since you'll be turning your head in a bunch of directions to see animals. A hat attached to a poncho ends up falling off every time you look up at a sloth. I always keep a rain hat in the car. It's not even the seventy-five-dollar mosquito-repelling hat I tried on at the adventure store before moving here. My dad gave it to me... and he probably won it in a Folgers coffee sweepstakes.

Playa Negra and Playa Blanco are two beautiful beaches worth visiting while exploring Cahuita. But remember my crime rule: leave nothing in the car.

Puerto Viejo From Cahuita, continue driving south until you find Puerto Viejo, the busiest of these tiny beach towns. Vendors line the beach and sell everything from jewelry to T-shirts. You'll find Puerto Viejo has everything you need for a fun vacation: bank, supermarket, internet cafes, restaurants, and affordable places to stay. It's also a popular hub for backpackers. Hostels here offer a wide variety of lodging arrangements: some rent tents, while others have standard rooms. Many backpackers take a break in Puerto Viejo before continuing their journey to Panama. Although you can find comfortable accommodations, you will not find a Four Seasons, Westin, or Marriott.

I've seen some of the most beautiful jewelry sold by vendors along the street. Another great souvenir is their locally produced chocolate.

Caribeans Chocolate Tour $28 | www.caribeanschocolate.com
Find out how chocolate is made! Learn about cacao and how

it's harvested, and find tropical wildlife that is part of this ecosystem. Don't forget to load up on lots of chocolate bars at their gift shop—the perfect souvenir for all your friends back home.

If you are looking for an active nightlife, remain in Puerto Viejo. But if you're looking to escape the crowds and experience more nature, continue driving.

Playa Cocles If you don't have a car, you can rent a bicycle or hire a taxi. It's a beautiful intermediate point between the quiet beaches further south and the busy nightlife you'll find in Puerto Viejo.

Caribe del Sur Tel: 2750-0202 | www.villasdelcaribe.com | The room are spacious, colorful, and air-conditioned. During low tide, an area right off the beach turns into the perfect hot tub. Thank you, Mother Nature.

Terra Venturas Tours $95 | www.terraventuras.com | If you're looking for excitement, stop by and take the Jungle Adventure Tour. Spend the next six hours rappelling, zip-lining, crossing hanging bridges, and hiking waterfalls.

Punta Uva Five miles down the coast from Puerto Viejo is one of my favorite beaches in the entire country. It has awesome reefs located only a few meters from shore. I've spent hours snorkeling here. It only takes a few steps into the water before you're witnessing schools of fish swimming around you. If you're lucky enough to catch a week without rain, the water transforms into a sparkling reef aquarium full of life. It's so clear you'll spot even the tiniest of fish lurking in the reef's crevices. And the best part is it doesn't cost a thing! I could spend days snorkeling here and never get bored.

Manzanillo is literally the end of the road. It's a small town with affordable lodging options and the famous Maxi's Restaurant

Maxi's Dine on a delicious seafood platter that will leave you stuffed for days. Or just order a drink and enjoy the Caribbean breezes. I've said this before and I'll say it again, the best things are often found at the end of a dirt road.

Gandoca Manzanillo Wildlife Refuge Digest quickly because there is another great reef for snorkeling right off the coast. Or skip the snorkeling and continue straight ahead into the forest. The paths within the park wind you through a lush jungle. Eventually, you'll come to a point where you can walk out onto a ledge and see the famous Manzanillo Rock. This scene is breathtaking and appears on countless postcards in souvenir shops. You know you're succumbing to the Caribbean vibe when a rock makes you happy.

There are affordable accommodations in this area, and some even have air conditioning. If you're the type who enjoys sloths more than people, Manzanillo is the perfect place to escape from it all.

White-faced Capuchin Monkeys

Southern Pacific Beaches

"Waves are toys from God."
~ Clay Marzo

From Jacó all the way to Uvita, you won't want to miss this incredible stretch of beaches. There are jungles and waterfalls, zip-lining and sport fishing. There's even a river of crocodiles, just in case that's on the list!

Getting There

If flying into San José, take the Autopista del Sol (Route 27, also known as the Caldera highway) all the way to Orotina. Once you pass Orotina, look for the Jacó/Tarcoles sign and merge onto Route 34 (the Costanera Sur). From here, it's 45 minutes to Jacó.

This coastal highway is one of my favorite drives in the country. Traveling with a dense forest to your left and an ocean to your right invites daydreams of cracking open a coconut and lounging in a hammock.

Tarcoles River As you make your way toward the Southern Pacific beaches, you'll pass over a bridge with many people staring over the edge. Underneath this overpass are humongous crocodiles. This has become quite the tourist attraction, but don't climb down the bank to get a closer look. Crocodiles are sneaky and strike quickly.

There was a time when this was a prime spot for car theft, so be aware. They have stationed police here, but keep in mind that anything left in your car anywhere in Costa Rica may not be there when you return.

Carara National Park $10 | 7:00 a.m. to 4:30 p.m. | Just a short distance past the Tarcoles River on the Costanera Sur is the Carara National Park. It offers three trails, one of which is wheelchair-accessible. I always recommend hiring a guide since they're better at spotting wildlife. If you're lucky, you'll see the scarlet macaws that nest here every year. But don't worry if they elude you! I've spotted them simply by sitting on the beach.

The Beaches

Playa Herradura The popular Los Sueños Resort is located here and is one of the first beaches you'll encounter. Approximately a mile and a half north of Playa Herradura is Playa Leona. Although this beach appears to be blocked by hotels, you can access it by looking for an unmarked dirt road.

Los Sueños Marriott Resort Tel: 2630-9000 | www.marriott.com | One of the more opulent places to stay. This is the spot to get pampered! There's a big pool and a great swim-up bar, and it's only minutes away from some of the best fishing in the country.

Jacó One of the more popular towns in Costa Rica, Jacó is packed with restaurants, souvenir shops, and hotels. Although not one of the most scenic black-sand beaches, it's a known surfing spot and a great place to plan excursions. At one time it had an unsavory reputation, but things are changing, and today you'll find a larger police presence. There's a scenic bluff just past the town where you can take incredible pictures of the Pacific. And scarlet macaws are plentiful!

Tortuga Island www.adventuretourscostarica.com | Accessed by boat from Jacó, Puntarenas or Montezuma, this island is the perfect excursion. Many take off from Jacó, which is a 90-minute trip. Snorkel, hike its wildlife refuge, or lounge on the beach. Contact Adventure Tours and ask about their catamaran package.

Jacó Laguna Resort & Beach Club Tel: 2643-3362 www.jacolagunaresort.com | When you just have to be beachfront. This moderately priced hotel has a great pool and clean air-conditioned rooms.

Playa Hermosa (the southern one, not the beach in Guanacaste) One of my favorite beaches, only eight minutes south of Jacó, is Playa Hermosa. It's where I first witnessed scarlet macaws flying overhead. Costa Rica is constantly unfolding its beauty, often when I need it the most. Nature has a way of fixing the things in me that need fixing and reminding me to slow down and look around. After seeing those birds, I knew I'd be living in Costa Rica for a long time.

Playa Bejuco About 20 minutes south of Hermosa is Bejuco, a beach that can be easily missed. It's like the busy town of Jacó and is a quiet place where I took the cover picture for my first book: that cute little doggie waiting for his owner to come back from surfing. I felt like this dog while working in my office: waiting for something that would spice up my life, like a wave that would surge straight toward me. Unfortunately, that didn't happen. I finally realized that life would not surf to me; I had to paddle out toward it.

Hotel Playa Bejuco Tel: 2779-2000 | www.hotelplayabejuco.com | Rob and I had a great stay here while traveling down the coast. It was a good night's rest, followed by a morning walk on the beach. It's a good memory, one that reminds me of why I moved here in the first place

Playa Palo Seco Fifteen minutes further down the coastal highway is the town of Parrita, Watch for the turnoff to your right for Playa Palo Seco. This beach is on a small peninsula that borders the ocean on one side and an estuary on the other. Don't miss this barrier isle. It reminds me of Gilligan's Island, with rows of shady palm trees and scores of sand dollars peppering the beach. This tract of land is so narrow, you feel as if you can skip a stone right over it from the estuary to the sea. The water is quite rough, but if you're looking for a quiet place, one where you rarely see anyone on the beach, you should add this tiny piece of paradise to your itinerary.

Manuel Antonio Do you like monkeys? Do you feel like there's not enough of them in your life? If that's the case, Manuel Antonio is the place for you. Monkeys run this town.

Manuel Antonio National Park $16 | 7:00 a.m. to 4:00 p.m. | It's not the biggest park in Costa Rica, but what it lacks in size, it makes up for in wildlife. You'll see three out of the four types of monkeys that live in Costa Rica: howler, grey-capped titi (squirrel), and white-faced (capuchin). The titi is endangered, but they are easy to find in the park. White-faced monkeys are the most mischievous. Don't be surprised when you see them pickpocketing tourists while they stare up at the canopy. They'll steal anything: cigarettes, money, and—their favorite—shiny keys. It's not uncommon to see a frantic tourist chasing the monkey as it swings from tree to tree, hoping that he'll drop the keys.

When visiting the park, don't forget to pack a swimsuit. Several white-sand beaches provide the perfect place to unroll a towel and relax. We were on one of these beaches when a couple of raccoons robbed us. Seriously, we watched from a healthy distance while they ransacked our backpack.

Hotel La Mariposa Tel: 800-572-6440 | www.lamariposa.com | This Spanish-Mediterranean hotel is mesmerizing with its incredible ocean views. Gosh, it's a pretty spot, and it's where I saw a white-faced monkey chase away their bartender. The monkey wanted cherries that were in a bowl on the bar. He charged and made himself look huge by standing tall and stretching his arms into the air. The takeaway: let monkeys have the cherries.

Sí Como No Resort Tel: 2777-0777 | www.sicomono.com | The perfect place for families. With their views, their lounging monkeys, and their incredible pool, everyone in your party will have a great time. They also implement sustainable policies to reduce their impact on the environment.

Hotel Costa Verde Tel: 2777-0584 | www.costaverde.com | A wonderful place to observe monkeys, splash in their cliffside pools, or just enjoy a cocktail while admiring the panoramic ocean views. This hotel is also famous for their 727 fuselage suite! That's right, spend a night in a retrofitted airplane. Or grab a drink at their C-123 Fairchild cargo plane, now converted into a pub. There's a whole Sandinista story behind this. Check out their website to find out more.

Cute Fact: White-faced monkeys are named "capuchins" because their caps of hair resemble the cowls of Capuchin monks.

Dominical Approximately 45 minutes from Manuel Antonio is Playa Dominical. If you're a surfer, you already know this tiny beach town is popular for its dependable waves. It's also a place where you'll find the same animals that are up north, but with a twist. Red iguanas lounge overhead on sunny branches, and fiery-billed toucans dine on palm fruit all along the coastline. It's as if they sprinkle Dominical with paprika; every animal is a little jazzier than its counterpart found in other parts of the country. Every time I'm in Dominical, I'm amazed at what I see each time I look up.

The town is made up of only a few unpaved streets, lined with restaurants and shops. I've never seen anyone rushing here. And why would they? This place is designed for relaxation and surfing.

I never sleep better than when I'm in Dominical. Rob and I spend lazy mornings watching iguanas climb trees and toucans flying overhead in search of breakfast. Surfers paddle off in the distance, hoping to land that perfect wave, and fishermen prepare for their day by catching bait in the bay before heading out to sea. It's so incredibly peaceful, it's hard to remember how rushed I used to be and how anxious my mornings were. Maybe that's the reason I sleep so well in this small town: I know I'll be waking up to a masterpiece.

Dominical smells good too, like a forest of fresh-cut grass. It alive and hopeful. It softens your hard, pointy edges created by years of stress, sanding them down little by little before ultimately creating a smooth curve. Stress sticks perfectly on pointy edges, but with curves, it has nowhere to rest. Bad days thoughtlessly slip away.

I've seen some amazing sunsets in Dominical: orangey-red with bits of blue mixed in. The afterglow lasts a long time, with purply clouds resting on the horizon before surrendering to the night. Costa Rica is never shy when unveiling its loveliness.

Nauyaca Waterfalls About six miles from Dominical is one of the most beautiful tiered waterfalls in Costa Rica. It rises 200 feet into the air. From its entrance you can either hike the 2.5 miles or reach it by horseback. Swim in the pool at the base, or take your chances and jump from its cliffs.

Uvita Sixteen minutes south of Dominical is the tiny village of Uvita. It's home to the Ballena Marine National Park ($6 per person). From July to November and December to April, you'll see whales off the coast. The view from overhead reveals how the beach forks, and its outline actually resembles that of a whale's tale. What a coincidence!

Cano Island A beautiful snorkeling spot only an hour and a half by boat from Uvita. You don't want to miss this. It's one of the best spots to snorkel in all of Costa Rica.

Osa Peninsula

"I think it's time to ask yourself:
what do you believe in?"
~ Indiana Jones

Osa is home to one of the few remaining lowland tropical rainforests in the world. The crown jewel of this peninsula is the Corcovado National Park, spanning over 103,000 acres. National Geographic once called this area "the most biologically intense place on Earth." Can you imagine that? A unique setting overflowing with wildlife? Costa Rica is a treasure chest, eager to sparkle once you crack open her lid.

Puerto Jiménez is a great jumping-off point. From here, you can plan many excursions, even ones into the heart of the park. Or, you can fly straight into the isolated Drake Bay and enjoy being in one of the most remote spots in Costa Rica.

Corcovado National Park

There are no words to describe what it feels like to hike through this jungle. Home to over 360 species of birds and 140 mammals, this park is jam-packed with wildlife. You'll see all the types of monkeys that reside in Costa Rica: howler, capuchin, spider, and the red-back squirrel monkey (a member of the titi family). I've seen more scarlet macaws here than in any other part of the country. Their yellow, red, and green feathers sweep the sky like iridescent kites.

You might get lucky in the park and encounter the endangered Baird's tapir. It's a funny-looking animal: part pig and part cow, with a splash of rhinoceros thrown in for good measure. They're nocturnal, so the odds of seeing one are small. Your best chance is to wait near a watering hole. On a hot day, you may find one submerged with only his head above the water.

Although I've never seen a tapir, I came across a path lined with dozens of snakeskins. I was startled at first, but later relieved. I would much rather step on a snakeskin than tread across the actual snake. It was hard to tell which species left these skins behind, mostly because I didn't stick around long enough to find out. There are enough poisonous snakes living in this jungle to persuade me to skedaddle: coral, bushmaster, eyelash pit viper, and the infamous fer-de-lance (also known as the Costa Rican landmine). When there are snakes nicknamed after explosive devices, you know it's time to move on.

Getting There

Flying SANSA has flights that land in either Puerto Jiménez or Drake Bay, the latter of which borders Corcovado National Park. I always say, the best things in Costa Rica are down a dirt road, or in this case, down a dirt landing strip.

In this particular zone of the country, the air is overstuffed with oxygen. Microscopic particles of wonder buzz around you, creating a force field of curiosity. You'll feel like a child again, uncovering the marvels of this planet, seeing bugs and plants you never knew existed. This rainforest is one of the biggest gifts Costa Rica shares with the world.

Know that when flying into Drake Bay, you should have already reserved a place to stay. The area is known for its ecolodges deep in the middle of the jungle. From here you can plan your hiking trips into the park.

Driving to Drake Bay If flying is not an option, it's possible to drive to Drake Bay. But be aware that it's most likely impossible during the rainy season due to several rivers that have no bridges. Even in the dry season, you'll need a four-wheel-drive vehicle with high clearance.

The start of this trip is similar to the drive to the Southern Pacific beaches. From San José, take the Autopista del Sol and merge onto Route 34 (the Costanera Sur). Another option is to take the Pan-American Highway from San José, continuing south to San Isidro del General. This will take just under three hours. Once there, turn right and follow the signs to Dominical, where you can get onto the Costanera Sur.

Continue on the Costanera Sur until reaching the town of Charcarita. Stop at the town's gas station to fill up; there will not be another one for a while. Turn right at this gas station and continue driving for approximately 45 minutes to Rincón. Just before the bridge, make another right and follow this dirt road for an hour all the way to Drake Bay.

Another option is to drive to Sierpe. Park your car at the Las Vegas restaurant. From Sierpe, it's a 1.5-hour boat ride to Drake Bay.

The lodging in this area is eco-friendly. There is no air conditioning and spotty internet.

Hotel Las Caletas Lodge Tel: 8826-1460 | www.caletaslodgedrake.com | Enjoy the sights and sounds of the jungle in Drake Bay! It's the perfect spot for seeing the park. Just remember that you're away from civilization, and all the creature comforts of home may not be available. But who comes to Costa Rica to binge-watch *Stranger Things* on Netflix?

Puerto Jiménez If you're not interested in traveling to the very remote Drake Bay, fly or drive straight to Puerto Jiménez. Don't turn off at Rincón, but continue following the signs to Puerto Jiménez. This small town is packed with incredible things to do. Some of the best excursions are trips to the park, mangrove tours, and fishing adventures.

Puerto Jiménez borders the Gulfo Dulce, the bay that separates the peninsula from the mainland. Here you'll see many dolphins and it's a great place for snorkeling.

Agua Dulce Beach Resort Tel: 2290-4100 | www.aguadulcehotel.com | Within Puerto Jiménez is the beautiful Playa Platanares. This resort sits just steps away from this beach. I have some of the best memories of staying here. The number of scarlet macaws flying around this property is breathtaking.

Rob and I sat under an almond tree as they ate the nuts above us! We got pelted with shells but didn't care. We were mesmerized by the colors on their wings, a crazy blend of saturated blues, reds, and yellows. These birds are pieces of flying artwork.

There is an indescribable feeling of contentment all over Osa Peninsula. It makes you want to see more of Costa Rica and the rest of this amazing planet.

Kayak Tour and Adventures Tel: 2735-5195 | www.aventuras-tropicales.com | One of the more spectacular excursions is a guided mangrove kayak tour. The water is so flat, it reflects the sky like a watercolor painting. They have a great fleet and are about the most knowledgeable people in the area. They will point out the abundance of wildlife: carpets of crabs, blue herons, white ibis, black hawks, and monkeys.

The owner told us a hilarious story about capuchins that constantly break into his garage and toss tools around. You think your neighbors are annoying? Try living next to a gang of monkeys.

As he told this story, I was thinking I should update my crime chapter to include monkey theft. I then shared with him a disgruntled email I received from a man who moved to Costa Rica after reading my book and ended up living next to an annoying rooster. He even demanded his Tico neighbor get rid of his rooster.

"Are you the woman who wrote a book about moving to Costa Rica?" the guide asked.

"Yes, I'm her. Why?"

"I'm that Tico neighbor!" he laughs. "This guy moves next door and tells me that he read a book about a lady moving to Costa Rica. It inspired him to move here as well. After a week, he starts coming over and complaining about my rooster. I could understand why he was upset, since my rooster is a little confused. He crows all night. But he wanted me to kill the bird and I refused. To me, my rooster sounds beautiful. It made my neighbor so angry he went down to the municipality multiple times to complain."

"So what happened to the neighbor?" I asked.

"Oh, he moved."

"And the rooster?"

"He stayed."

I can't be a hundred percent certain that I was the author the neighbor was talking about, but it does sound a little suspicious. To think that by happenstance, I would be in the middle of a mangrove tour with the notorious Tico rooster neighbor is hilarious. I'm glad that my books are bringing people closer together, only to have them move farther apart.

Scarlet Macaw

Happier Than A Billionaire

It's been four thousand days since we landed in Costa Rica, and I can still remember things about that first week. Like the sound of rain hitting the dark pavement when we walked out of San José Airport, and the windshield wipers of our rental car barely keeping up with the downpour. The smell of kitchen cabinets made from Guanacaste wood. The weird dish soap that comes in a solid block. Eating blackberries off the vine. Rob holding my hand, his thumb rubbing against my skin as if to make sure I was still there.

These reflections are like feathery puffs on dandelions. As a kid, I'd make a wish and blow; the white fuzz hoisted its seeds along air currents like tiny parachutes. It was then I realized how far a breeze can take something small and light, and how an object so white could later turn into such a magnificent yellow blossom. Blowing these seeds around may explain why so many dandelions grew in our front yard. But I loved our flaxen-speckled lawn and could never understand why people tried so hard to eliminate them. Who decided to call them weeds, and why are they not worthy of being admired? I think they're beautiful. My parent's lawn was, and still is, a yellow masterpiece.

The best thing about my life in Costa Rica isn't the grand adventures, as most might think, although I've had plenty over the years. The best thing is that no day is like any other. Living in a place, that in a way, still feels foreign. There have been a million moments, stacked on top of one another like tiny Lego blocks; little bricks of happiness reconstructing a new life in a new land.

Since the day we set out to explore an uncertain future, a force lifted me off my feet. It was as if little champagne bubbles were pushing me upwards. The more I moved away from my old life, the more the effervescence of this new one tickled my toes. Feeling weightless is a strange sensation, especially when I'd never realized how much weight I'd been carrying around.

Lift is the aerodynamic force that directly opposes weight, and it's what keeps paper airplanes up in the air. To generate enough lift to fly, there must be lower average air pressure at the top of the vessel than on the bottom. Rob is the lift that got us here; it's his lower pressure that changed our trajectory. He knew that to get up in the air, we needed to decrease our drag, manage our weight, and provide the right thrust. None of that happened immediately. It turned out our obstacles took us on a scenic route. And what a scenic route it's been.

Your adventure will be unlike any other: a story surrounded by different colors and sounds and laughter. The scenic route is easy to miss if you concentrate on all the things that can go wrong, and doing that is like sinking in mental quicksand. The easiest way to avoid it is to keep your eyes wide open along the journey. It was when I stopped squinting that I had the most soulful, funny, batty events occur. I remember them all, and I neatly display them in my head like bowling trophies on a fireplace mantel. They might not be Olympic gold medals, but they're shiny just the same.

So take your dreams and unpack them every night. Call your friends—the ones who already know you're crazy—and tell them what you're planning to do. Turn to your spouse at night and play the "what if" game.

What if we left?

What if it didn't work out?

What if it did?

Each "what if" is a fold, and every day you're one step closer to your goal. A "what if" conversation is where it all starts, and it's what got us here. And then follow it with "How bad can it be?" My husband's go-to response whenever he sees me having a panic attack.

Hopefully, this book has given you the confidence to go out and create your own escape plan. You can do this. I know because I did it and I hardly knew anything. I'm still a little bewildered by it all. And feeling bewildered is a fun feeling to have.

Jim, you can now close this book since you've got some work to do. Find your passport and check the expiration date. You'll be traveling light, so grab the carry-on. Explain to Hazel you're taking her on a trip where you'll stand on top of a volcano, then sit under a palm tree, and end the day watching a sunset. Tell her how pretty she looks in the moonlight and that her laughter is the sweetest sound in the world. If she still wavers, ask her, "How bad can it be?"

It's not bad at all, Hazel. Living in Costa Rica feels like a three-day weekend. Like that Monday morning when you realize you still have one more day to yourself. You don't jump out of bed but instead stretch out and feel the softness of the sheets and coolness of your pillow. Three-day weekends always feel unexpected. Few people ever wake up on that third day and say, "Wow, I'm already bored." They're always blissfully wonderful. I bet more people fall in love on three-day weekends. I'm certain it's when most children make wishes before blowing on dandelion puffs.

In those four thousand days since moving here, Rob and I made paper airplanes. Simple ones at first. We folded every crease and tossed each into the wind. Many landed at our feet while others veered sharply to the right. But there was one that Rob cast perfectly. It hitched a ride with a parrot before flying over a waterfall. As I watched it climb higher and higher, a current rose underneath and lifted me ten feet into the air. I heard the sound of the rain when we first landed in Costa Rica, smelled the kitchen cabinets made from Guanacaste wood, and tasted those blackberries picked fresh off the vine. While hovering, I glanced down and there was Rob, keeping the air pressure just right so that I could fly.

He reached up and took my hand, holding on tight, rubbing his thumb against my skin, as if to make sure I was still there.

The End

Happier Than A Billionaire: An Acre in Paradise

(First Chapter)

BURRITO MAN

"I'm starting a burrito business," Bobby says while standing under a palm tree. "I'm calling it... are you ready... Bobby-Ritos." He splays his hands in the air as if revering a neon-lit Vegas marquee. To seem polite, I look up as well. I do not splay or revere.

Tonight, people are approaching me with the very first thought on their minds. They pick me straight out of a crowd or corner me in the bathroom. Apparently, I wear an expression of someone who is keenly interested in what others have to say. Most times I am. But not tonight.

So far I've been approached by an expat who—because of my big, stupid face—felt the pressing need to confess that he's in charge of covert operations at the Pentagon. That tête-à-tête was a walk in the park when compared to the gringo who, moments ago, sounded the alarm that the United States government was currently herding its very own citizens into internment camps. Right now... as we speak.

"They are coming to get us, they are coming to get us," the man yelled.

Of course, this concerned me. I may not be versed in all current affairs, but surely this was something I needed to investigate further. I asked Paul Revere, who was one Corona away from falling face first in the dirt, "When are they coming? When are they coming? Are they headed to West Palm Beach? Browsing Lake Tahoe? Will the internment camp have a pool and a meal plan? Because frankly, that doesn't sound all that bad." The man nodded and glanced up at the sky, most likely summoning the mother ship.

However, Bobby doesn't appear inebriated or crazy. He isn't wearing an aluminum foil beret and did not mention one internment camp. This is a deliberate career strategy.

"I'll be selling burritos full-time. That's the biz I'm in," Bobby says, putting his hands on his hips while rocking back and forth on his heels.

"So you moved from the United States to Costa Rica, and your plan is to sell burritos? In a Latin country that is already proficient in the art of encasing food in tortillas?"

"That's right," he confirms, using a tone normally reserved for inviting applause. According to Bobby, this Fortune 500 idea has early retirement written all over it.

I've never seen someone so happy to open a burrito business. Come to think of it, I've never seen someone so happy, period.

Bobby reaches into his pocket and hands me a business card. The logo is a smiling, blue-eyed burrito, overflowing with sour cream, guacamole, and a cheesy sauce dripping over the side. The cartoon looks delicious.

"Contact me for any and all of your burrito needs." Bobby-Rito then tips his imaginary hat and exits under his equally imaginary marquee. I'm left asking myself, how many burrito needs can one person have?

Rob steps down from the stage and lifts his guitar strap from around his neck.

"Who was that?" Tonight was supposed to be a relaxing one, watching my husband play guitar on the beach.

"A burrito salesman. Odd business choice, don't you think?"

"I don't know. It's not the worst idea," Rob says.

"Come on. It's strange. Of all things, burritos?"

"Why do you find it so odd?"

"He's calling his business Bobby-Ritos. And he already printed out business cards." I grab the one from my pocket to show him.

"Aw, the logo is adorable. Come on, give the guy a break. I freakin' love it!"

Rob is always urging me to grant people breaks, but usually, it's him who is requesting one. This commonly occurs when I change the television station to any reality program, specifically one with women screaming at each other.

"So, because the blonde didn't invite the brunette on an Atlantic City spa vacation, she tossed wine in her face?" he said as I explained the complexities of reality show female dynamics. "That's just Thanksgiving Day in Brooklyn. Give me a break, Nadine."

Rob has been asking for these breaks for as long as we've been married. He's requested so many over the years that I began asking him how long each should last. Should he be left alone in the living room for a few hours, or would he prefer I pack him a weekend bag? Apparently, they are herding people into internment camps, so I'm sure I'll be able to flag down the next shuttle bus.

"When you think about it, Bobby-Rito is no weirder than us," Rob states. "We did the same thing he's doing, short the guacamole. He probably had a crazy job in an office somewhere and dreamed of doing something completely different."

"You could be right. Or he could be nuts. I've met a lot of nutty people tonight."

"Either way, when you break it down, all of us expatriates are Bobby-Ritos."

Can this be true? Are we all Bobby-Ritos? Rob and I did sell everything we owned and moved to Costa Rica. No one said it was a good idea. My parents wholeheartedly did not think it was a wise decision, but Rob and I knew we had to go. The thought of spending the rest of my life in an office was sinking me into an abyss of depression, which for me meant being irritable ninety-nine percent of the day. That, in turn, resulted in Rob steering clear of me one hundred percent of the time.

Rob grabs his amp and hands me his guitar. "Let's get out of here. We've got a long day tomorrow."

He's right. It's going to be a long day because we're moving once again. The time has come for us to say goodbye to our rental house. Our landlord decided to put it up for sale, and we are moving into a different place about fifteen minutes away. Every time we move, I go through a delusional process of denial.

"I'm not doing it. They'll have to drag my cold, dead body out of here."

Rob ignored me and wisely began calling property managers. "It's not going to happen!" I scream over his shoulder.

The main reason I don't want to leave our house is that it's where I photograph hundreds of howler monkeys right from our balcony. Mature trees surround the home, and monkeys climb straight up to its windows. This allows me to take the most remarkable pictures of their faces and hands, as well as video of them cramming lavender flowers into their mouths. I've watched babies jump on and off their mothers' backs, and males fighting for dominance before falling asleep seconds later.

For the longest time, the monkeys congregated across the street in a neighbor's yard. I waited patiently, howled at the right times, and tossed a few bananas outside, only to learn howler monkeys don't eat them, iguanas do. And once the iguanas finished the bananas, they turned their sights toward my husband's baby hibiscus plants. I call this the circle of life, or things a wife never admits to her husband.

"Where the hell are all these iguanas coming from?" Rob yelled after finding yet another plant eaten down to the stem. I just shrugged my shoulders and acted bewildered.

But I never gave up, and soon it happened: the monkeys came to my side of the street. And once they did, I never wanted to live anywhere else.

It's not only the monkeys that I love so much about the house but also the birds: trogons and mot-mots, white-throated magpie-jays and squirrel cuckoos. I even spotted a painted bunting: a bird that often hides in dense brush. My backyard is a perennial aviary.

One morning, I glanced out my bedroom window and saw a huge anteater jumping from branch to branch searching for a termite's nest. He stuck his snout into the air, concluded that none were around, and disappeared back into the canopy. That never happens in New Jersey, and if it does, I can assure you that's not an anteater loitering outside your bedroom window.

"I feel like we move a lot. Maybe too much," I say.

"You have to look at it as an adventure. Almond trees surround our new rental. Can you imagine all the parrots we'll see? It's going to be great. Plus, there will still be monkeys. Maybe not up to our window, but we'll still hear them every morning."

I exhale. "You're right."

"And we'll be right next door to Sandy and Ian. Having our friends so close will be a blast."

I like the idea of living in the same community as my friends. Our cars regularly break down, and one of us always needs a ride to German mechanic. We all spend a lot of time there.

Ian is a cool guy. While out in the ocean, Rob once accidentally yanked the plug on Ian's inflatable kayak. Ian took a drag from his cigarette, blew smoke signals in the air, and casually said, "I guess we're going down." That's the most excited I've ever seen the man.

I am also eager to live closer to Ian's girlfriend, Julieta. She's Costa Rican and doesn't understand much English, and Ian is American and doesn't speak much Spanish. But they've been together for years and enjoy each other's company more than most couples I meet.

It's endearing how Julieta always addresses him as "my love." When we're at the grocery store, I can hear her call over the aisles, "Need café or leche my love?" Or while waiting for him in the parking lot, "I missed you, my love." I once told Rob that I thought it was sweet how they spoke, so he started calling me hotpants, which doesn't have quite the same romantic ring when called across the produce aisle.

"Hey, hotpants, where are the bananas?"

I like spending time with Julieta. She's tall and voluptuous, and ine every picture we take together I resemble her Raggedy Andy doll. I even started practicing cooking authentic Costa Rican dishes for her, like my fried plantains, which turned out to be fried bananas. She smiled and ate them regardless.

Julieta tries so hard to understand my crappy Spanish, and I try so hard following her lousy English, we both spend a sizeable amount of time squinting at each other. Our friendship is unquestionably ruining our eyesight.

However, the number one thing I like about Julieta is she is a wizard when dealing with bureaucratic red tape. Can't get your driver's license? Julieta will speak with the clerk. Want an extra ten percent off your deep fry cooker? Julieta has got it covered. I've never met a woman so persistent.

"I know the new rental will work out. It always does," I say. "But the house is down such a long, bumpy dirt road it rattles my brain."

"But what do we always say? Everything that's great in Costa Rica is usually down a dirt road. Look on the bright side; we'll be right next to the beach. We can kayak and snorkel all the time now. Trust me. How bad can it be?"

(Read more about our adventures building The Happier House in *Happier Than A Billionaire: An Acre in Paradise.*)

People You Want to Know

My Backyard Mechanic 8638-1238 (Guanacaste Area) | Whether you're stuck on the road, in your driveway, or just ready to get rid of that clanking sound under your car, Rigo will come to you. He also works on scooters, ATVs, and motorcycles.

My German Mechanic 8887-1447 | Horst can handle all of your needs with the precision one might expect from a German mechanic.

Painter and Drywall 6030-6228 | g.valencia.mig@gmail.com | If you live in Costa Rica long enough, you are bound to deal with heavy rains and clogged gutters. This may lead to drywall and paint issues. Call David and his father Carlos Gonzalez for any job, big or small, throughout the country.

Cesar the Pool Guy 8711-0622 | For the best prices and service in everything pool related, call Cesar. He will give you an honest deal.

Gardening 2665-8470 | www.cocobolotreefarm.com | Whether you'll looking for fruit trees, ornamental plants, or ground cover it's hard to beat Cocobolo.

Spanish Teacher 8729-4857 | www.spanishforexpatscr.com | Boy, do I have the Spanish teacher for you. Sylvia at Spanish For Expats will get you speaking the language in no time!

Dr. Andrea 2653-9911 | http://beachsidemedicalclinic.com | One of the best doctors in the Flamingo area.

Dr. Candy Midence 2446-7440 | dra.candy@lineavitalcr.com | Excellent doctor in Atenas and has helped many expats.

Accountant 8319-4691 | pbrenes@ultimateconsultingcr.com | If you plan on doing business in Costa Rica, you'll need a good accountant. Call Pricilla Brenes in Tamarindo.

All things real estate, including rentals 8423-4370 | (US) 630-280-1985 | ginab@ginabhomes.com | If you are looking to move to Costa Rica, Gina Briguglio can assist you in your housing quest!

Budget Traveling If you're a hostel hopper and bus rider, contact Donavan at www.facebook.com/365CostaRica. He can help you plan a budget trip!

Concierge Services 8863-9964 | (US) 615-713-2205
www.costaconcierges.com | Located in Atenas, Costa Concierge Services can assist you in property management, rental properties, rental cars, and more.

Index

A

B

C

D

R

S

T

X

Y

Made in the USA
Middletown, DE
23 June 2020